CULTURE & POLITICS

by Ronald Berman

NIVERSITY
PRESS OF
AMERICA

LANHAM • NEW YORK • LONDON

University Press of America,™ Inc.

4720 Boston Way
Lanham, MD 20706

3 Henrietta Street
London WC2E 8LU England

Printed in the United States of America

ISBN 0-8191-3706-5

Cover design by Elizabeth Dixon

All University Press of America books are produced on acid-free paper which exceeds the minimum standards set by the National Historical Publications and Records Commission.

DEDICATION

For Barbara, Andrew, Linda, Julie and Kathy

ACKNOWLEDGEMENTS

A number of people have been kind enough to help me with this book. I am grateful to Armen Tashdinian of the National Endowment for the Humanities for his assistance in providing materials and to Roger Rosenblatt of TIME for going over the manuscript. The Rockefeller Foundation gave me a summer stipend to work on this book, and the expenses it entailed were supported by the Smith Richardson Foundation. I am especially grateful to the Smith Richardson Foundation, and to its Director of Research, Leslie Lenkowski.

TABLE OF CONTENTS

PREFACE

This book is a record of the development of the National Endowment for the Humanities from 1972–1976, the years of my term as Chairman of the agency. It is also a commentary on federal policy on arts and humanities. It is based upon the following sources:

Hearings before the Committee on Labor and Public Welfare, United States Senate, 1971–1976.

Joint Hearings before the Special Subcommittee on the Arts and Humanities of the Committee on Labor and Public Welfare, United States Senate and the Select Subcommittee on Education of the Committee on Education and Labor, House of Representatives, 1973–1976.

Hearings before a Subcommittee of the Committee on Appropriations, United States Senate, 1972–1976.

Hearings before a Subcommittee of the Committee on Appropriations (Interior and Related Agencies), House of Representatives, 1972–1976.

The Congressional Record, 1971–1976.

National Foundation on the Arts and the Humanities Act of 1965 (Public Law 209—89th Congress) as Amended Through December 4, 1980.

Humanities (Bulletin of the National Endowment for the Humanities), 1971–1976.

Annual Reports to the President of the United States from the Chairman of the National Endowment for the Humanities, 1971–1976.

Also taken into account are unpublished records, minutes of proceedings, correspondence of the Office of the Chairman of NEH, journals, memoranda, and program materials.

CHAPTER I

The National Endowment

The establishment of the National Science Foundation in 1950 indicated to part of the academic profession that it could rely on the federal government for subsidies. And indeed the sciences were able to count upon national support. Their success provided an example for the humanities. In the attempt to emulate the sciences, and to keep some kind of parity with them, historians, philosophers and literary critics campaigned for federal patronage. They became a constituency.

The humanities, like the sciences, succeeded in attracting the attention of government. In part that was due to the great expansion in education after the admonitory flight of *Sputnik*. By the late fifties it became generally accepted that education was a national mission: that the schools produced what the nation could use. If we are to follow the Department of Commerce publication, *Social Indicators 1976*, between 1950 and 1975 the national percentage of the age group 18–19 enrolled in colleges and universities doubled, going from about 18 percent to about 36 percent. By the end of the seventies, according to the Department of Health & Human Services, there were about twelve million students enrolled in higher education. This meant not only that more campuses would have to be opened, but that large numbers of teachers would have to be recruited. Many more people were involved in the profession of teaching by 1975 than had ever been the case before. And the hundreds of thousands of teachers in the humanities had new and rising expectations.

The American Council of Learned Societies expressed the aspirations of a new and potentially powerful class when, in 1962, it urged the formation of a new institution:

This Council very strongly urges that the Federal Gov-

> ernment, in the national interest and for the strengthening of our scholarly and intellectual resources on the broadest possible front, extend its support of higher education and research to include all the humanities and the social sciences on the same basis as mathematics, the natural sciences, and technology.

In order to embody those aspirations a National Commission on the Humanities was founded in 1963 which recommended to President Lyndon Johnson the establishment of a federal endowment. The report of this commission emphasized that funds for the humanities should be channelled through existing institutions. Individual beneficiaries would be teachers and scholars: corporate beneficiaries would be colleges and libraries.

Understood in these limited terms, the report won a small number of supporters in Congress. The report was discussed by the 88th Congress in August, 1964 and received national attention when President Johnson responded to its hopes and implications in a speech delivered at Brown University in September. In this speech, the President stated his personal support for what would eventually become a new federal agency. As he put the matter, "The values of our free and compassionate society are as vital to our national success as the skills of our technical and scientific age." The idea of a new federal agency appealed to the Great Society: during the first weeks of the 89th Congress, 76 bills were introduced to establish such a foundation, co-signed by 40 members of the Senate and 105 members of the House.

In the course of discussion certain issues were raised without being resolved. The House asked what was to be done with another new constituency asking for subsidy, that of the visual and performing arts. The question was, should every aspirant to federal support receive its own little agency? Most members of Congress thought not, and debated instead the desirability of joining arts to humanities in some kind of symbiotic relationship.

There were issues felt to be even more basic, among them

the question of whether government had the responsibility to do anything at all about culture. There was the matter of defining the exact degree to which art or scholarship might be said to contribute to the national welfare. And one of the themes of congressional discussion was the possible opposition of the general public to programs of such narrow interest.

However, after long debate, both House and Senate passed Public Law 89–209 in September, 1965, which authorized the existence of the National Foundation on the Arts and Humanities. This foundation was to consist of two sister agencies: the National Endowment for the Arts and the National Endowment for the Humanities. The two were to be autonomous. They were to have separate staffs, independent budgets, and their own Councils or board of trustees. Each agency was to have its own Chairman. And each was to have its own field of operation. The National Endowment for the Humanities was to be responsible for supporting the study of the following:

> Language, both modern and classical; linguistics; literature; history; jurisprudence; philosophy; archaeology; comparative religion; ethics; the history, criticism, theory, and practice of the arts; those aspects of the social sciences which have humanistic content and employ humanistic methods.

The two endowments began by sharing $5 million for their first year of operation, although provision was made for additional matching funds in the event that they could obtain gifts from the private sector. Barnaby Keeney became the first Chairman of NEH to serve a full term, but, because he could not leave Brown University before the end of the academic year he was preceded by an interim Chairman, Henry Allen Moe, President Emeritus of the John Simon Guggenheim Foundation.

Although Barnaby Keeney was to serve only a single four-year term his administration proved to be decisive for the agency's development. By 1966, the first year of his term, basic programs of the agency had been identified and a bureaucracy organized around them. There were to be three main operating divisions of the Endowment: Fellowships, Research and Publication, and Education and Special Projects. In order to handle the large amounts of paperwork made necessary by the annual submission of a budget, a fourth division, the Office of Planning and Analysis, was also established.

A professional staff was assembled which, over the entire history of the agency, was to provide bureaucratic expertise and continuity. Procedures were established emphasizing several stages of review for applications: perhaps the most important of these was the formation of boards of outside reviewers from the academic world.

Keeney began the endless round of consultation with members of Congress which is necessary for the health of any federal agency. He was successful in arousing the sympathy of key leaders in the House of Representatives like Albert Quie of Minnesota and Frank Thompson of New Jersey. The best indication of the agency's good relations with Congress was its moderate but steady growth. In 1966, the two Endowments had shared the original appropriation of $5 million. In 1967, NEH received as its share of appropriations $2 million; in 1968 the figure for NEH was $3.5 million; in 1969 it was $3.7 million; in 1970 it was $6 million; in 1971 it was $11 million. By 1972, after Keeney's departure, the budget went up to $24.5 million.

Finally, Keeney paid particular attention to the appointment of a workable Council. The enabling legislation of NEH calls for a 26–member National Council on the Humanities. Membership is "on the basis of distinguished service and scholarship or creativity." The legislation also stipulates that the Council shall represent both the learned professions and the general public. From its earliest days the Endowment took the law to mean that members of the Council should represent the humanities in general rather than constituencies—or even institutions—in particular. Appointments were for the most part made on the grounds of scholarly distinction and academic experience. Equally important, a regular schedule of quarterly meetings was devised which called for the active participation of the Council in setting policy as well as in the review of applications.

In its first five years the agency enjoyed the services of a good staff and went through a period of moderate but steady growth. There were, however, some incipient problems. First and most important was the restrained enthusiasm of Congress for the humanities. Both authorization and appropriations hearings had indicated that while there was a minority in the House and Senate which actively promoted the two endowments the majority might be said only to tolerate them. The purposes of the two agencies were often misunderstood, and sympathy for them was not extensive. When the Arts Endowment made some unpopular grants its appropriations were quickly cut.

The second major problem had to do with the Humanities Endowment in particular. Those academics who had served on the Commission for the Humanities had a fairly traditional view: they intended that the agency's annual budget be spent on academic affairs. And yet, this was a national agency. The members of the House Appropriations Subcommittee came from states with few major universities. So far as they could see, their votes enriched other states already better endowed. They naturally looked for other kinds of patronage opportunities, and urged the endowment to channel its funds more equitably. It did Nevada, with one university, no noticeable good to insure a constant flow of academic rewards to Massachusetts.

As the opposed interests became more plain the chairmanship of Barnaby Keeney was marked by continuous argument. The agency hoped to fulfill at least some of the expectations of Congress, while its academic constituents resented any prospect of diverting funds from their original and narrowly-conceived purposes. Keeney was constantly lectured by professors who feared the loss of funds for research, and by members of the House who wanted some kind of payoff for their support of a relatively friendless and vulnerable agency. One group wanted to subsidize a profession; while the other wanted to equalize the flow of benefits among and between the states.

The last problem that afflicted Keeney and his successors was a matter of definition. We recall that the American Council of Learned Societies had, in its resolution of 1962, argued for support of the humanities "in the national interest." But, in after years, not only was the idea of the national interest subjected to differing interpretation—so was the identity of the "humanities." One element of confusion was the relationship of the humanities to (or their difference from) whatever might be humane, humanitarian, or of general human interest. Everybody among the constituents of the two endowments wanted something, and each individual desire was naturally reflected by congressional interest. Throughout the history of NEH there has been a profound difference of opinion about what the agency should do, and about the benefit of what it does.

For example, congressional debate in the beginning and over the years has stated that cultural support in the way of appropriations for the two agencies should be diffused as far as ghettos, hospitals, schools and neighborhood centers. There must, according to Congress, be some *practical* benefits from the operation of NEH and NEA. Their grants should enhance rural life; make teenagers less destructive; illuminate the golden years of senior citizens; awaken ethnic pride; and raise the national consciousness. To judge from the many expressions of congressional concern over the years, "art" refers to the art of living and "humanities" refers to human problems.

Even the idea of the "national interest" has undergone a fascinating change. The original constituents of ACLS understood the phrase to mean the support of research in history, literature and philosophy. But even sympathetic members of Congress wished to believe that the phrase meant something more. For example, Senator Claiborne Pell of Rhode Island, who has been more influential than any other man in formulating the law governing NEH, has long believed that the agency's funds should be distributed not only by region and by state *but to individuals.* In 1964 he made the first of innumerable allusions to the work he really wished NEH to undertake: the donation of small grants of $500 each to "grocers" and "lumberjacks" who might wish to acquaint themselves with serious reading. Over the years, in discourse on the subject, his King Charles' head has been the Scandinavian woodcutters who read Racine through the long nordic night.

And of course by the late sixties another historical moment had arrived. One of the consequences of campus unrest was the anxious haste of nearly all universities to prove their moral and political virtue. This took the form of asserting that many traditional disciplines, like those of the humanities, were no longer important. They mattered less than the study of those things which were nearer to political activism or minority interest. The idea of the national or even of the educational interest changed notably in the world of education itself.

In 1964 "the national interest", at least as the phrase was used by the ACLS, suggested professional research in the disciplines of the liberal arts. By 1965 the phrase contained new implications: it was in the national interest to provide the Great Society with agencies embodying its accomplishment. In 1966, after prolonged congressional debate, the phrase meant the widespread dissemination of benefits to a national electorate. And, after the activism of the late sixties, there were new meanings for the idea to absorb. Here, for example, is the 1968 statement of the National Council on the Humanities on the new mission of the agency:

> The present crisis of American society leads the National Council on the Humanities to reaffirm that the humanities ideally are always relevant to the condition of man, and of man's society. It therefore wishes to encourage, in addition to significant studies and works in the familiar humanistic tradition of pure scholarship and general knowledge, appropriate project proposals within the various fields of the humanities which are concerned with values as they bear on urbanization, minority problems, war, peace and foreign policy; problems of governmental decision, civil liberties, and the wider application of humanistic knowledge and insights to the general public interest.

As we move from the original implications of "the national interest" to those of "the general public interest" we move from post-war to post-modern expectations. Certain questions are bound to be raised by this extraordinary display of hopefulness. Among them, is it possible that the humanities can do *anything* about war, peace and foreign policy? Or does the adoption of such language mean that the agency itself is much in doubt as to the work it does, and the effect it looks for? After the publication of this resolution the Endowment was routinely beseiged by applications from those certain they could solve the problems of national life if they but had grants to do so.

It is implicit that some subjects are more equal than others. There is not much in this resolution about scholarship or education; but there is a great deal about the issues concerning Lyndon Johnson's Great Society. The work of the agency, one senses, is to be validated only insofar as something is accomplished which will bring about peace or equality. The resolution says nothing about what may happen to any agency which fails to affect such large undertakings. Nor does it seem aware that an agency devoted to such differing ends may well develop what we sometimes call a crisis of identity.

CHAPTER II

Being Nominated

With the departure of Barnaby Keeney in 1970 the National Endowment for the Humanities went through a period of disorganization and self-doubt. For a period of almost two years one difficulty came after another. The White House attempted to appoint a successor, but the attempt ended in a well-publicized disaster. The President's choice was an able and intelligent writer, Stephen Hess, who was justifiably well-regarded by the White House staff. But Hess was not an academic. He had no doctorate, and was not employed by a university. The appointment was bitterly and successfully attacked by the American Council of Learned Societies. After many hostile letters had accumulated in the Personnel Office files his nomination was withdrawn: an embarassment both for the administration and for the agency. One side-effect was the alienation of Congress, which became as suspicious of the Nixon administration in regard to the National Endowment for the Humanities as it was of other national issues.

There was no successor for almost two years. Although NEH was ably led by Deputy Chairman Wallace Edgerton it could not hope to have the attention of the President—hence of anyone else in Washington—without being led by someone appointed by him. During 1970–71 two things had become plain: NEH was being outstripped by its sister agency, whose support of the visual and performing arts gave it enormous visibility and popularity; and it was unable to take any initiative in programs which might attract media notice and congressional interest. The agency had become a poor relation in a city which valued only power and access to it.

From 1970 on the National Endowment for the Arts made repeated attempts to sever its connection with the hapless Humanities Endowment. Its Chairman, Nancy Hanks, believed that there was only so much money in the federal till for culture, and that if the Arts were free of the inhibiting presence of the Humanities then it would inherit the larger share. She was, I think, correct. The Arts Endowment had very quickly become the congressional favorite for a number of reasons. It served large audiences and it did things comprehensible to anyone who watched a performance. It had a fantastically good press. And it was backed by hundreds of institutions well experienced in lobbying for funds. In fact, the Arts Endowment became a model, at least in congressional eyes, for the performance of the Humanities Endowment which was also expected to reach large audiences and generate wide and visible public response to its grants. The cornerstone of my own policy was to be the absolute refusal of the Humanities to be separated from the Arts. The difficulties of association notwithstanding, if the two agencies had been severed there would have been a very large Arts Endowment and a very insignificant Humanities Endowment.

In August, 1971, the White House Personnel Office notified me that I was being considered for Chairman of NEH. I was invited to Washington and took part in a long series of interviews which lasted until November. In the course of discussion I was asked to criticize the past performance of the agency, and to state how I would improve it. That was difficult to do from the outside but, after going through many files I did become reasonably fluent in tackling the issue of the agency's split identity. I suggested that it had to deal both with its traditional constituency and with the general public. It was now too late for NEH to view itself as having sole responsibility to academe. I added that the agency ought to become known for something more remarkable than the distribution of funds. Most cultural institutions—certainly most universities—were at that time in a good deal of a mess. In the attempt to placate the activism of the left they had changed their curriculum and disavowed much of their authority. It would be good, I said, if the Humanities Endowment could return some self-respect and confidence to education. In time, the practice of granting academic credit for taking part in political campaigns or for opposition to American culture and government might be discouraged.

I also pointed out to those who interviewed me at the White House—Leonard Garment, Patrick Buchanan, Frederick Malek, Raymond Price and John Clarke—that the Republicans had so far not won many friends in the world of ideas. Those who taught, thought and wrote were by now accustomed to look to the Democratic Party for encouragement and advancement. And certainly they looked to the Democrats to translate their ideas into public policies. One of my arguments was that NEH might allow the Republican Party to have more contact with intellectuals than it had in the past, for there were hundreds of thousands of men and women in the world of education and ideas.

Those who interviewed me were naturally concerned with the state of things at the time. America in 1971 had just emerged from a kind of civil war. That war had taken place within the institutions of culture. In 1964, those institutions had been hallowed; but by the end of the decade few had kind words to say for even our greatest universities. A soundly-run Endowment for the Humanities might help a great deal to normalize relations in our national domestic life.

The principal responsibility for selection of a Chairman of NEH lay with Leonard Garment, who had been associated with Richard Nixon's law firm in New York City. Garment was then a leading figure on the White House senior staff, responsible, among other things, for culture, minority affairs, and for whatever infusions of good sense the administration could tolerate. We had many long talks about the future of the agency, and agreed in most of our views about it. Garment worked hard at getting the principal Senators on the nominating committee to agree with the President's choice. This was not an easy job. Jacob Javits of New York and Claiborne Pell of Rhode Island were very much in charge of the Arts and Humanities. In part, that was by default: they undertook to support and oversee these agencies in an indifferent Senate, and in return were allowed considerable freedom of action. The administration had for two years done very little to establish its own claims to leadership. Both senators would have preferred a liberal candidate familiar and agreeable to them. They were unhappy with my choice and put up a four-month long resistance to it. But they were worn down eventually; as Javits later explained to me, his own inquiries in the academic field could not reveal anything damaging. I was helped by Barnaby Keeney, who recommended me to senator Pell.

There was an audible sigh of relief in the academic world when it was announced that a Shakespeare scholar would be nominated for the job. The American Council of Learned Societies made no trouble, and *The New York Times* welcomed my nomination. Many academics took part in the inevitable formality of writing letters on my behalf. With these in hand, a file could be maintained in the White House with which to forestall opposition. There was in fact no opposition, although the Committee on Labor and Public Welfare remained unsatisfied. The hearing took place on November 30, 1971, the same day on which a new Director of the National Science Foundation was also nominated by the President. Guyford Stever received *pro forma* attention from the committee while I was subjected to something more inquisitive.

Javits began by reading a passage criticizing the New Left from a recent book of mine, *America in the Sixties*, and demanded to know whether radicals would under my chairmanship be excluded from public benefits. I responded that of course they would not be excluded; and that in any case the New left was now much less radical than it had been, many of its representative figures having been absorbed into academic life. And I added that the agency would welcome any and all applicants. I was then asked whether Norman Mailer, whom I had criticized in *America in the Sixties*, would be eligible for a grant from NEH; I replied that he would probably not need one. Throughout the questioning Javits was hostile—for which he apologized handsomely and in public after his first year's experience with the new management. But the experience was after all consistent with university life, in which the apparition of a conservative reasonably equipped with morals and ideas brought forth astonishment and suspicion.

Senator Pell avoided political issues and suggested that I contemplate "little grants to little people" in order to diffuse the benefits of the humanities. He had been struck, in a previous conservation, by my idea of expanding the agency, and he directed discourse to that point. Perhaps the crucial moment of the hearing came up then:

> Senator Pell: At about what do you see the level of authorization of your program at the expiration of your term of office; what would you like to see it?
>
> Mr. Berman: I am tempted to bring in the example of the Duke of Urbino. It was said of him, in praise, that half the income of the state was spent on libraries. I don't think we will reach that point, but I would hope we would approach the $100 million figure anyway.

It was rather a startling sum of money for an agency which at the moment had about a quarter of that, and few prospects for increasing it. It remained, of course, to convince the administration that such funds could wisely be spent; to extract them from Congress; and to figure out what to do with them.

Before any of that could take place I had to decide certain other things. After confirmation by the Senate, early in December, 1971, I began to think about strategy and tactics. There were, it seemed to me, about a dozen things that had to be done before the agency could expand. First of all, the President would have to be personally involved in any plans for development. Without his consent the Federal Budget would never include any new funds for NEH. I relied on Leonard Garment to interest the President, and to get me access to him.

Clearly the next thing would be to win over the subcommittee of the Senate committee on Labor and Public Welfare. At present its leading figures, Senators Pell and Javits, had no confidence in the administration and little in me. Yet they were responsible for authorizing the legislation of NEH: every three years they wrote a bill which set the limits for the agency's purposes, and the limits on the money that might be spent upon them. As a stranger to Washington I was unknown to them and as a conservative I was distasteful.

Equally important, the sub-committee on Interior and Related Agencies in the House would have to be won over. Of all congressional committees this was the one most closely connected to the two Endowments. It conducted a rigorous annual hearing into their activities and was responsible for their appropriations. This sub-committee was also chaired by the Democrats. In addition to all other complications, its members were mostly from the far western states, who had chosen this committee because it had the oversight of the Department of the Interior. They were primarily interested in the management of state parks, and in land, mining and timber rights. Finally, they had no particular reason to admire the humanities, or to wish well those eastern states which had many universities, libraries, and other potential beneficiaries of NEH.

As for the agency itself, new programs would have to be designed to absorb new money. These programs would support not only universities but other cultural institutions, for example, museums. And they would certainly involve television. I wanted especially to attract media coverage, since Washington responds to the press almost as obediently as it does to the electorate. Every agency in the city knows precisely where it stands in the world by the tone and weight of its clippings.

The permanent staff of the agency would have to be expanded. It would also have to be educated. I wanted a staff which would share my views and carry them out, a rarity in Washington. But I should say in advance that my greatest success came here: converting bureaucrats already in place and attracting good men and women who made the agency an expression of their talents.

There were finally a number of tactical ends. NEH funds would, I knew, have to be concentrated in order to accomplish any good. The temptation to do otherwise was there, for the Arts Endowment had made it a practice to give out innumerable little grants in order to wet every beak. There was an advantage to this, for it prevented organized disaffection. But it kept every grantee in a state of uneasy gratitude, pleased to have money yet annoyed to have so little of it. There was a high degree of friction in the relationship of NEA to its constituents. I decided not to follow that example: instead I would concentrate the funds of NEH into large and useful projects. I would avoid subsidy. And I would try to convince my own constituents that it was better for them to think professionally than it was to think institutionally. I gave myself even odds at best, and went after the first target of opportunity, President Richard Nixon.

CHAPTER III

Getting Money

The general arguments I had made to the White House senior staff were augmented by an argument even more formidable, made by Leonard Garment to Richard Nixon: it was that great national leaders had throughout history patronized the arts and the disciplines of the humanities. Garment was a friend of countless writers, artists and musicians. He was deeply cultivated himself. He realized that culture was to become a national issue: not only the passage of ideas but the confrontation of styles. He knew something about patronage, was concerned about the rising costs of performances in the arts and of research in the humanities, and he was alive to the times. He could see that intellectuals, if not a class in themselves, were a new, large and vigorous force in American society. He convinced Richard Nixon that public policy should make provision for this reality. And he made it his business to take the existing framework of legislation governing NEA and NEH and make it into something able to bear a considerably heavier weight of intention.

Leonard Garment arranged for me to see the President. The interview worked out well. Richard Nixon was noticeably hostile to intellectuals, and grew more so during his term in office. But he treated me with forbearance. It seemed almost comical to him that I should suggest benefits for him by providing them for his adversaries. But he was willing to listen and even, to a certain extent, to go along with my ideas.

We got along well, and I think that this was something of a factor; less important though than the presence of Leonard Garment who had arranged our meeting, and who knew how much it might mean. We talked about books and history for quite a while—the President was at least momentarily pleased to run across someone in the administration aside from Garment and Raymond Price who read books that interested him. He was himself omnivorous. It was clear that, like John Kennedy, he knew something about nineteenth-century history. He was especially interested in revolution, and in the consequences of 1789 for cultural life. He viewed the French Revolution with horrified respect.

If the interest of John Kennedy centered on the art of rule and on figures like Melbourne, that of Richard Nixon seemed to rest on the expression of national policy. If we are to judge by the memoirs that both he and Henry Kissinger have published, that interest was in early 1972 natural. The National Endowment for the Humanities intruded upon his attention while he was thinking about the Chinese Summit, the Soviet Summit, and the invasion of the DMZ by North Vietnam. I did not know what was on his mind concerning these things, but we did talk about the changes that had made modern times. And we talked a great deal about books that made those changes intelligible. After the meeting I would occasionally send the President notes about things we talked about, and now and then I sent copies of books to him: Edmund Wilson's *Patriotic Gore,* Elizabeth Longford's life of Wellington, Glazer's and Moynihan's *Beyond The Melting Pot.*

My main business was selling the agency to the man who could do most for it. I raised four points in my conversation with the President, some of which I had first explored during my interviews with the White House staff. The first of these had to do with the isolation of Republicanism from the intellectual mainstream—or rather, from some of its most turbid and interesting currents. The administration now had the equivalent of a Republican foundation which would be judged by what it achieved. If there were Republican cultural ideas, now was the time to test them. Did we want to become identified with academic freedom? With high educational standards? With the best or only with the most popular kinds of art?

The second point concerned education specifically. Universities throughout the country had lost both self-confidence and public standing. And within them, the humanities especially had lost part of their professionalism. The disciplines of the liberal arts were rapidly becoming identified with what felt good and seemed relevant: with encounter sessions for credit; with street-corner politics; with anything but their original subjects. Anyone who took ideas seriously would be pleased to help institutions that were first-rate or wished to become so; to raise standards and do the best possible educational job for the nation. If the President admired books and ideas then the best thing for him to do was to support the disciplines of thought.

The third point involved ways to reach the public. The university was not the only institution serving and transmitting ideas. It was accompanied by museums, libraries, research institutes, historical associations—and now by the press and television. There were clearly new institutions in the making, and new relationships to be established. It was entirely possible that large audiences outside the universities would become interested in what the humanities had to say.

The last point involved culture itself: the way that people thought about ideas, institutions and themselves. I took Mr. Nixon's election in 1968 to mean that something had happened beyond the usual presidential Olympics. There had been a kind of cultural reversal in America, and it was plain that the seventies would in some ways react against the decade preceding it. It was now becoming desirable for students to study, universities to teach, and politics to enlighten. Eventually all periods lose their force: the Restoration became boring; the *belle époque* became boring; and the sixties were now boring. American culture was now in the process of change—a change which I thought of as normalization. We are not a nation of extremes, and invariably look back upon moments of extremism as a departure from our ideals of behavior. If NEH were in tune with cultural change it could represent the best and most productive aspects of national life; it would stand for intellectual and moral seriousness. It is an unromantic notion, but not without excitement.

The important thing about seeing the President is that it was a public event. The visit was meant to be communicated. And of course it was: the Washington newspapers carried the story and implied that the agency had some new bargaining power in its adversary relationship with both Congress and the Office of Management and Budget. The staff of NEH was stimulated into life. And that might have been the most important side-effect of this episode, because in Washington nothing matters more than access, and nothing is more inspiriting than the knowledge that an agency has been, almost as if by magic, empowered actually to do its job.

After this, I was invited to see the Vice President in order to describe my plans, ideas and whatever insights about American culture I could manage. Although Spiro Agnew has become known for the disasters of his policy and character, there was more to him than that. He was in a sense bookish. He was interested in ideas and even in scholarship: a sociologist who had recently been in to see him told me that Agnew knew a good deal about a good deal more than politics. In our conversation, the Vice President wanted to know about New Left and Old Right; about the way I thought the seventies would look; and about the relationship that cultural activities had—or did not have—with the Republican Party. All I can say is that I found him personally agreeable and politically informed. He was no enemy to NEH, and that eventually was what really mattered.

Having won the support of the Executive it remained to win that of Congress. That had to be done almost immediately because the appropriations process for the new fiscal year ending in 1973 was already under way. Unlike authorization, which is concerned with legislation and takes place every three years, appropriations or funding hearings take place annually. And it is at these hearings that agency heads confront their real audience, perhaps their masters, those members of House and Senate who determine how much money will be spent.

The most important audience to which NEH played was the House Subcommittee on Appropriations, Interior and Related Agencies. It was headed by Julia Butler Hansen of Washington who, as chairman, had nearly absolute powers. Those powers are not always engaged and they are sometimes questioned, but there is more to them than writers of constitutions suspect. It was the highest of all art forms in Washington to win over a committee chairman.

Julia Hansen was wily, rational and businesslike. She could see the political influence of the Arts, and was willing to give the Humanities a run for the money. I think that she gave NEH a fair deal, given the agency's lack of pulling power in Washington, Utah and Nevada. She was fair enough, even though she had a marked preference for the Arts, was more or less impossible to lobby, and developed every hoop-jumping muscle that I had.

I've noted that the members of the House Subcommittee on Appropriations were almost without exception from states having economic interests in forests, rivers and dams. They had few cities and were lightly populated. And, they had frontier frames of mind. Selling arts and humanities to this group was always interesting. The members of the committee over the years of my term were colorful, clever, opinionated and willing to listen. But I had to argue for culture as a kind of public benefit, and that is the way the record shows it. The members were not entertained by ideas and they did not vote funds without some pragmatic purpose. They wanted large numbers of voters to benefit visibly. They were very shrewd and very inquisitive. In short, by no stretch of the imagination would they tolerate (or stay awake for) arguments couched in the traditional terms of academic discourse. I respected and liked them enormously.

This first hearing had a question that was to appear endlessly in every kind of future discussion:

> Mrs. Hansen: Can you define humanities for the committee?

It was a startling question, because Congress had done just that in the National Foundation on the Arts and Humanities Act, Public Law 89–209. The definition of the humanities was as old as the agency, it was emblazoned on its paperwork, it was forever alluded to—and it seemed to be completely unknown to those who funded the agency. I had what I suppose could be called either a blinding moment of illumination or a classical double-take when the question was asked: *because the definition of what we did was useless.* It could never satisfy Congress, which had simply adopted it from academic lobbyists who in turn had absorbed it from college catalogs:

> The term "humanities" includes, but is not limited to, the study of the following: language, both modern and classical; linguistics, literature; history, jurisprudence; philosophy; archaeology; comparative religion; ethics; the history, criticism, theory, and practice of the arts; those aspects of the social sciences which have humanistic content and employ humanistic methods. . . .

No matter what the virtues of the original Act, its language evidently contained nothing about the history, meaning, or function of these things. It implied nothing about ideas or values. In short, there was nothing to interest a group of delegates from Utah, Oregon and Washington who wanted to know what the humanities meant, and what the agency did.

I didn't allow them more than thirty seconds to find out. From that one question came the stock in trade of the agency's congressional relations over the next five years.

I began my response by talking about the common experience of anyone who has been to high school in this country. Congressmen go to school like anyone else and respond to the books they read, the ideas that seem important, and the things that move them. I asked the members what they remembered from school—how they had been taught, and what passages from the books they had read still stuck to them. I talked about the work of Mark Twain, who had managed to say a great deal about the part of the country they came from—I reminded them that he had written about Nevada and California as well as Mississippi. I asked them if they thought his kind of writing meant anything, and why. And I reminded them that was a society that might have to lean rather hard on what it remembered from Mark Twain. We no longer had some of the institutions he wrote about and we needed: church, community and family were now much weaker than they had been even in our own youth. Because of that, it was through books and within schools that many of our social values were now formed.

As for the definition, we certainly had to begin with the language used by Congress back in 1965. But we all knew that it was unsatisfactory, that in fact the members were only confused if not bored by it. But no one can feel any special affection for a telephone-book list of disciplines. I thought that the members of the committee were right to be bemused, and that they needed to relate books to lives. So I talked for a while, in the second half of this ad lib lecture, about the life of Samuel Johnson. I told them what I in fact believed, that the humanities began—as they did for Johnson—with the most intense curiosity for the lives of men. I suppose that I really asked them to think about why Johnson and Milton had their names on so many public buildings in America, while Sam Rayburn was one of the few members of the House who ever got one of his own.

The members were happy to see their intentions clarified. The lecture became a standard component of all hearings that were to come.

The main point of our subsequent discussion was that I was asking, in the name of this new definition, for almost double the amount ever before given to the agency. My purpose in that room was to get $40 million. And after explaining why it was being requested I had to come up with programs that would spend it.

I began my argument, as I had with the White House staff and then with the President, with the assertion that the Humanities could serve a public role. Not only were there many more people involved in teaching, not only had the student population more than doubled in the past decade; there were now many more institutions of education in every congressional district in America. There were large numbers of new kinds of institutions like Junior Colleges and Community Colleges. In short, there were many people who could use the agency's services.

In order to accomodate this new constituency, one of the

programs of the Endowment already most favored by Congress, the State-Based Program, could be revised and improved. This program had in fact been born at the insistence of our congressional committees. It was strongly backed by Senator Pell, who wanted the agency to diffuse its benefits among the general public rather than concentrate them at universities. In effect, the State-Based Program was a system or regrants; NEH appointed committees in each state which then subdivided an annual appropriation from the agency into dozens of local awards. This meant that Congress got visible local results, which is what it wanted so badly. Because the program had familiar political contours—it involved many people, numbers of whom were leading citizens in the various congressional districts—it was eternally popular on Capitol Hill. There was a similar program in the Arts Endowment, administered with much more political clarity. The Arts had to give away a stipulated percentage of their annual funds to state committees in the Arts, and there was no possibility of rejecting applications. The advantage was that such committees acted as influential lobbies for the Arts—the disadvantage was that they were dangerous rivals for federal funds. Eventually, they would absorb amazing amounts of money into bureaucracies of art; money that would be used, as Dick Netzer has remarked in *The Subsidized Muse,* only to lobby for more money.

The Humanities Endowment was able to set up its own voluntary committees. The members were not employees or appointees of state government. The criteria for membership were professional: nominees were recommended by local libraries, colleges, and historical societies. The applications for NEH funds turned out by such groups could be rejected by the parent agency. The funds given to them were not mandated by Congress, but voted by the Council of NEH. In short, the agency maintained control.

I proposed to expand the funding for this purpose while keeping its structure exactly as it was. This was one way in which to absorb new funds while assuring Congress that a proportion of them would go for the understandably political purposes of regional satisfaction. But, it is important to note,

NEH then and thereafter resisted the idea that its state committees should become as political as those of the Arts Endowment. We wnated the money, if it had to be distributed regionally, still to go to libraries and campuses. They might be local libraries and not the Folger or the New York Public, but they were still humanities institutions.

There were two other major expansions. NEH had already been involved in some television by covering the distribution costs of Sir Kenneth Clark's series on *Civilisation.* It was now time for the agency to become involved in programming. I had in mind a good deal more than a single series: a whole sequence of television programs which might rival the Masterpiece Theatre. This would translate the humanities into public form and give the agency what it badly needed, access to the media.

The beginning was small, but out of this initiative were to come the *Adams Family Chronicles,* the great BBC version of *War and Peace* and other important television programs.

In return for these public blessings I asked for a much expanded program in academic fellowships. A member of the NEH staff had come up with an idea for something we called Summer Seminars for College Teachers. It was destined to become one of the Endowment's major programs because of its simplicity and usefulness: being intended to move teachers from small campuses without facilities for research to great universities which would undertake to re-train them. Small classes of these teachers would meet under the direction of experts in their field. They would have a chance to do work of their own, and then to institutionalize their ideas in courses at their home schools. It was a cheap and large-scale enterprise which could quickly transfer the benefits of universities to places which needed development, but had no chance of affording it.

The hearings were blessed with assent, and the show moved to the Senate Subcommittee on Appropriations. There, much of the same was said, with much the same result. But the anxiety of Congress was evident in the unhappy tones of Senator Bible, its Chairman, who somewhat plaintively asked,

"And that will cost more money?" The transcript does not show his nearly audible wince. We were warned that congressional generosity does not come easily; and that exponential growth for a federal agency could be achieved only at a certain cost. If the administration wanted this initiative, it might have to be forthcoming on certain other things. As for NEH, it had little to trade, so that it might be caught between the larger forces of the Executive and the Legislative branches. But, the good news was that Congress was not disposed to interfere with the agency's growth—only to make something of it.

CHAPTER IV

Kidnaping the Bicentennial

No matter how sympathetic the administration might be to the idea of expanding its cultural agencies there remained a formidible roadblock: Congress was angry with the Nixon administration in 1972–73 because the President proposed to cut domestic programs, even to freeze certain funds and return them to the Treasury at the close of the fiscal year. The members were in no mood to honor his requests while having their own turned down. The mood of Congress, especially in regard to NEH and NEA, was best stated by John Brademas, Chairman of the House committee which oversaw our legislation:

> I alluded earlier to a bill that has been introduced by a number of us, including, I think, all the Members of the House of Representatives who are here today, that would provide $450 million over a 3–year period for each of the two endowments. . . . Well, I raise that question, of course, in view of the almost savage slashes, by the administration, in a wide variety of domestic programs. And the doubling of the budget for arts and humanities, which I said earlier I very much applaud, means that we in Congress are going to need some kind of general idea of where the administration sees itself heading in terms of budget requests for the arts and humanities.
>
> Because I have already found, in private conversations with colleagues who are strong supporters of the arts and humanities programs, a good deal of bitterness, to be very candid about it, in respect to the proposal to double the arts and humanities budget at the same time that funds for health, education and pollution control are being cut.

This was in part true. Congress hates to cut and loves to spend. What it would have liked more than anything was to have spent more on everything. At any rate, the President's cuts in domestic programs gave the House a convenient stick to beat us with. We were a program popular with the administration; hence a useful hostage.

There was one other political variable at that time, and it proved to be the most important in the history of the two agencies. That was the arrival of the Bicentennial.

The Bicentennial was now less than three years away, and it was already something between a tragi-comedy and a scandal. It had become the natural object of every conceivable kind of commercial speculation. Part of it might be pleasant enough, with two centuries worth of July Fourth celebrations. But the event would clearly never survive its own celebration. The Bicentennial was clearly fated to consist of parades, of ten-foot birthday cakes with Minute Girls inside, of moralizing of a kind familiar to the reader of *Huckleberry Finn* and *Martin Chuzzlewit.* The Endowment was already in the loathsome embrace of businessmen with access to Congress or the Adminstration, who promised everybody gold-plated cufflinks in exchange for millions.

The media were enraged by the federal government's preparation or lack of it for the event. John Brademas made a number of addresses about the subject at hearings for the two cultural agencies, and was able to take the high ground of moral criticism over an administration which clearly had no idea of what it wanted to do; or how it wanted the event to diffuse comfort and glory for Republicans.

It was at this point that the most important event in the history of the two endowments took place. In a brilliant stroke of imagination, Leonard Garment put the two variables together, and determined that the Bicentennial would become the occasion justifying the expansion of the Arts Endowment and of the Humanities Endowment. Congress would be appeased, the media would be satisfied, the agencies would be expanded, the nation's birthday would be observed—and the Executive Branch would do something immensely worthwhile both for itself and for the nation.

Garment reasoned that what the Endowments already did could serve as a basis for celebration of the Bicentennial. NEH already did more than any other source to support the study of American history. The editing that it made possible of the papers of the Founding Fathers was already a kind of Bicentennial observance. And the two of us drew up a list of things which might in other ways conform to Bicentennial expectations. That included the exhibition of historical artifacts; the study of history itself; the editing of important national papers; the production of material from our archives. But the list included other and larger ideas, and central among them was the idea that the two Endowments would be the nation's birthday gift to itself. Rather than have the Administration go along with the plans of the Bicentennial Commission (whose current hopes were for the re-enactment of the Boston Tea Party in suitable costume) it would make a radical change in the kind of celebration to be held.

The strategy was to convince both Congress and the public that the funds which might be used to celebrate an occasion could be better used to create new institutions. All of the money that would otherwise have gone on parades or souvenirs would go to NEA and NEH. It would not be a one-shot affair; possibly the most important part of the strategy was the idea that benefits would go on until long after 1976. That is to say, the budgets of the two agencies would be enormously enlarged, and then remain in perpetuity at their new levels. This represented a quantum jump of imagination, in the consideration either of the Bicentennial or of the future of the two cultural agencies.

There was something of a tightrope to cross before all this could happen. The Bicentennial Commission had been a fiasco. It had in fact been responsible for many of the notions about celebrating two hundred years of national history by selling painted beer mugs or throwing tea into Boston Harbor. The Commission had to be tactfully ignored. Other agencies which by the dozen had also made plans to do something for the Bicentennial were to be discouraged. A new clientele would replace municipalities and corporations. And Congress would have to go along with the plan.

That last was harder than it sounds. For Congress was already annoyed and suspicious, reluctant even to fund the Bicentennial celebration for a single year, 1976. It would now be asked to fund two institutions, for a much larger sum of money, over many years in the future. Endless rounds of visits to Capitol Hill were implied. The same argument that Leonard Garment and I made to each other would now have to be made to all of the agency's committees. But that argument would have to be supported by another one which would account for the expenditure of funds after the Bicentennial had settled decently into the past. If NEH did in fact get $100 million more or less in perpetuity, how would that be spent?

It was at this point that I was able to bring to bear my plans for the support of large projects involving film, television, museums, and the exposure of humanities in other ways to the general public. The first of these was *The Adams Family Chronicle* which would prove, I hoped, that the endowment could get into the television business on a competitive basis. It would lead a long sequence of televised versions of American history, of short stories, drama and documentaries. I did not think then, nor do I now, that the use of media was demeaning to a cultural agency. Culture is always a matter of translation. It is not that movies and television are art forms—in fact, they strike me as boring. But they have the capacity to show fiction and non-fiction in ways that books don't. In any event, one must go where the audience is.

Museums would have to be reconsidered as potential clients of the Humanities Endowment. There were many of them, some incredibly large, and they served immense numbers of the public. Museums did work native to our interests, and could absorb a great deal of money. Until now our connection with them had been limited: NEH trained curators and provided some funds for educational programs. But the agency was now to enter the public arena of exhibition, and I intended our entrance to be striking.

One may wonder what the Humanities Endowment was

doing at all with museums, what possible connection it could have to painterly or plastic art. The museum program of the Endowment derives from a little-noticed line in the act of Congress which created the agency. That passage which defines the humanities includes the phrase, "the history, criticism, theory, and practice of the arts." It was a phrase long ignored, if only because of the natural assumption that the Arts Endowment contained everything of that nature in its own territory. But the history of anything is the province of the humanities, whether of ideas or taxes or science—or art. And it has of course been within the world of humanistic scholarship, in Berenson, Janssen and Panofsky, that the historical interpretation of art has taken place.

The Humanities Endowment was empowered to deal with every aspect of art except its creation. And so, in 1973, it began to do so. I was animated not only by the spirit of interpreting the legislation correctly, but by the desire to reach institutions which were in effect large markets for our business. And I was especially concerned to get some of that loving attention which our society confers upon art—attention which until now had been drawn only by the Endowment for the Arts.

The history of a remarkable enterprise, exhibitions of a kind and scale rarely done before, began with conversations in Washington and New York. Carter Brown of the National Gallery was interested in the joint funding of exhibitions and Tom Hoving of the Met was especially interested in shows with international scope. Out of these conversations came the exhibitions of the *Unicorn Tapestries, Soviet Modernist Art, The Chinese Exhibition, Scythian Gold, Late Cézanne,* and the *Treasures of Tutankhamun.* Sequentially they broke all world's attendance records, but that is not the way to defend them. They raised the level of public discourse and appreciation. They traveled to people and places far from Washington and New York. And, they showed that the humanities were interesting—that high culture was interesting, and did not have to be debased for general acceptance.

I suppose it could be said then that the two Endowments successfully kidnapped the Bicentennial and kept the ransom.

The hundreds of millions that were early intended for distribution to many government agencies found their way to these two. The definition of the Bicentennial was changed: it no longer meant the celebration of a single occasion but the extended activity of NEA and NEH. Leonard Garment had done something taking the combined talents of Willie Sutton and the Duke of Urbino.

Almost immediately a series of grants were made which translated our strategy into action. Three of them seem to me to have been historically important. The first began our great run of world exhibitions; it was for *Impressionist and Post-Impressionist Paintings from the USSR*. The title, cumbersome and not very revelatory, refers to the treasure of French paintings amassed in Russia before the Revolution and then hidden from public sight for many years because Stalin did not quite know what to do with them. The exhibition was made possible by a change of heart and policy in the USSR. It consisted of some forty works by Matisse, Picasso, Cézanne, Van Gogh and others from the Hermitage and Pushkin Museums. The paintings had been collected by Sergei Shchukin and Ivan Morozov just before the Revolution and indicated the character not only of French painting but of Russian society at the time. This was the first time in many years that the paintings were open to the West, and there was considerable awareness of that by the media.

The exhibition did some good for art and much good for the Humanities Endowment. The agency covered the cost of mounting, interpreting, and moving the collection about. And we began to put together a staff that would in the future come to be known for its expertise in the intricate diplomacy of art showings. After several years the agency was to conduct virtually its own foreign policy with the ministries of culture of other nations: discussing every detail of selection, packing, transportation and insurance for exhibitions.

A grant of more direct Bicentennial interest was made to the American Association for State and Local History for the production of a uniform set of state histories. It began just after the Soviet exhibition and, although designed for an audience just as large, it had other criteria in mind. There has never been a uniform edition of state histories in this country, nor have the possibilities of scholarship ever been fully developed. This project bought the services of people like Bruce Catton and Wilma Dykeman. And it linked them to an audience both professional and general. It was only after seeing the reception of the individual volumes as they appeared in the *Nebraska Sun* or the *Tennessee Times* that their effect could be appreciated. People are just as serious in the provinces; they just have less to be serious about.

The project certainly revived scholarship, for it made the writing of history into something of a marketplace event. And it focused the interest of Congress onto a project that was both academically sound and of genuine *regional* interest. Unless one works directly with the House of Representatives one forgets the power of regionalism. There is no doubt that the members have a national interest at heart, but that is rarely their first thought. What they want to see from the Executive Branch are benefits plain to a local electorate. And this history project, although it did not concern individual congressional districts, did the next best thing, which was to focus attention on the states.

In no respect were Bicentennial funds to be better used than in the third of the grants I have taken for examples. In 1973, the Department of Health, Education and Welfare had decided to cut off funds for libraries throughout the country. And, the Office of Management and Budget decided that the Humanities Endowment should not step in where a much more formidable agency feared to tread. In the view of OMB, library assistance was best left to municipalities. NEH had the temerity to disagree. It did so with full awareness of the absence of political benefits: research libraries are specialized; they are not open to the public; and although they serve great numbers, those services are not really visible to the public. Not many people know the names of these libraries because they are not attached to other institutions. They are on no state budget, and must become expert at private fund-raising. They are nearly always run at a loss.

Among research libraries there are about twenty million volumes and forty million manuscripts. Their collections are unique, and it is not really possible to do work in any of a dozen scholarly fields without making the pilgrimage to the Folger or the Newberry or the Huntington. And the greatest of these libraries—for example the New York Public—have thousands of users in the professions.

The New York Public Library was in fact to be a test case for the agency's interpretation of its mission. Although the administration did not wish to subsidize libraries, this one, like many others, was having a good deal of trouble in making ends meet. It could not even keep its doors open for several days a week. We evolved a rationale for assistance which was that it was on the face of it humanistic for such libraries to operate. And, that even though a library like the New York Public was conspicuously local it served a national purpose. I don't think the argument was likely to have been settled by reasoning, but it was settled by money.

The fact of the matter was that NEH had a large gift and matching program which was at that time something of an embarrassment. In 1973 the agency was entitled by law to match $3.5 million worth of gifts from outside sources. And, in that year as it most others it was very hard to find enough gifts to do so. In a sense, the New York Public Library conferred a benefit upon the Endowment by allowing it fully to utilize Treasury funds available. The Library had a staggering amount of users from corporations. It was used by tens of thousands of the general public. And it was one of the beloved institutions of its city. All this meant that it could raise gifts which NEH could match.

The Endowment gave half a million to the library and out of this developed an enterprise in the millions. The grant helped the library enormously—but it did two things important to the Endowment. The first was that it validated the idea that the agency could represent both scholarship and public utility. The second was that it allowed the agency to expand its gift and matching program so that literally millions of dollars could additionally be devoted to the humanities.

The New York Public Library managed to match the half million we gave it. The way it did so was interesting if not historical. Articles and editorials on the grant suddenly appeared in *The New York Times,* the *Post* and the *Daily News* all praising the agency and the Nixon administration. There was an outburst, very nearly a carnival of public support. Musical groups performed on the corner of Fifth Avenue and Forty-Second Street; benefits were held in more conventional places; the East Side Savings Bank advertised that it would no longer give electric toasters to new depositors but would instead contribute funds to the Library drive. As for that drive, it passed the half-million mark almost immediately, setting the stage for an even more ambitious campaign the next year. At Lincoln Center I was able to convey the congratulations of the President to a huge audience of donors which would on other occasions have been happy to string him from the chandelier. It suddenly became chic to support the humanities in New York, and to participate in their success.

All this aided the other programs of the agency. Because of it we were able to keep Congress and the administration quite happy, and to suggest that they give us money for fellowships and research. If the sister agencies had become the nation's gift to itself, what they did constituted a rather remarkable gift to the nation.

CHAPTER V

Making Grants

It has been said of the casual irresponsibility of government spending that, "a billion here, and a billion there—before you know it, it adds up to real money." Both Endowments now did aspire to real money; together they hoped to have a billion every five years. I began the 1974 budget hearings before the House Committee by asking for amounts which had before this been limited to the physical sciences:

> This budget proposes $65 million in definite appropriations and $7.5 million in indefinite funds to match gifts generated from private or non-Federal sources. The combination of Federal and non-Federal funds will make $80 million in new funds available to the National Endowment for the Humanities, compared with $41.5 million in the present fiscal year 1973.

The Committee was sympathetic, for by this time we had decent relationships not only with Julia Hansen but with the man who was to replace her upon retirement, Sidney Yates of Illinois. He and Joseph McDade of Pennsylvania, the ranking Republican, were to be of inestimable value to the agency. Without their work in committee and on the floor, in the corridors and in every other kind of negotiation, it would not have been possible to get a budget like this one off the ground.

The same budget was of course defended before the Senate Committee, which while also sympathetic was mindful of an impending conflict. One of the most fascinating things about democratic politics is the adversary relationship it forces between different programs caught by the limits of taxation. Social spending—or getting the money for it—is a kind of civil war. Senator Stevens, who had to get the money from the minority side, was very troubled by the increase, and Senator Bible accurately predicted a bruising floor fight in response to the virtual doubling of our budget while so much else in government was being restricted by the President:

> Senator Bible: My problem is a very simple one, and that is we can't build hospital beds for people who are sick because the administration freezes our appropriations. There is a great need for sanitary facilities all over the United States, and a modern bathroom is very desirable moving into the 20th century, I think. We are far behgind in that in many of the areas of the United States. We have our ghettos that we can see right from here, looking out this window, and we are trying to improve them and yet we can't get the dollars to do it.
>
> We want low-cost housing for our elderly and senior citizens because they are on fixed incomes and don't have the dollars to take care of themselves the way they used to. The dollar just doesn't go as far, we all know that. And yet they freeze public housing; we don't have the housing to put our elderly in, but the budgets are down in each of those instances. Now, Arts and Humanities is almost the only appropriation I have that I am handling—and I handle public works as well as Interior—where the budget has been increased; nearly everybody else has been decreased. This is the priority problem that bothers me, because we do have a ceiling and we have to meet that ceiling.
>
> So, I just wanted to think out loud with you and see what we could trade off for humanities. Would we trade off bathrooms or hospital beds, or medical attention, or a further assault on arterial sclerosis, or multiple sclerosis, all of which have been cut? Should there be more dollars put there and less dollars in your area?
>
> I am for your progam, and I have been for it right from the word go, and I think your record will show that I saved it once. We almost lost it on the House side. But I am just wondering whether this is the time or place in

> history to double when everybody else is being cut back; that is all I am saying, and that is our problem. You made your usual good appearance. We will just keep thinking out loud and conversing back and forth as we go along.

These wère serious issues for House and Senate and were to result in extended floor debate in which the two agencies would come up with spirited attack and defense. The immediate reasons for expansion were fairly plain: the President liked the two programs; the White House staff liked the media coverage they got; almost alone favorable among other government initiatives. Leonard Garment continued to support us in periodic debate with the Office of Management and Budget. The Arts constituency, composed of those who had both cultural and political influence, lobbied unceasingly for their own appropriations which could not but benefit Humanities. And the academic world, traditionally hostile to the Nixon administration, was now very much behind that part of his policy dealing with their own interests. Politically speaking, Arts and Humanities were rather hot items.

There was a larger context. *RN: The Memoirs of Richard Nixon* explains the opposition of the two branches in early 1973:

> It was clear that Congress was determined to do battle. Connally reported to me that the mood on Capitol Hill was "the most vicious thing I have ever seen. They are mean and testy." No sooner had the Vietnam peace agreement been announced than the complaints began over the re-organization plans, the proposed budget cust, the December bombing, and what was soon labeled as the attitude and style of the "Imperial Presidency."

There were other reasons for the opposition of the two branches. The President thought that Congress had become "undisciplined, isolationist, fiscally irresponsible, overly vulnerable to pressures from organized minorities, and too dominated by the media." As for myself, I didn't know whether we were looking at an opportunity or a bear-trap. We could be exempted from the restrictions placed on all other domestic agencies, or cut down in a way that expressed congressional feelings about the presidency.

The budget for 1974 was presented in a context of national oppositions. I did my best to reflect congressional sentiment because most of the function of the Executive branch is the persuasion of the Legislative. I am not sure that the following qualifies as taking the bull by the horns, but I tried to give our committees a way out of their own dilemmas. In response to Senator Bible and to the private questioning of members of the House, I argued that the activity of the Endowment was in fact social and that it should be considered as a natural part of our domestic programs. This was dangerous ground because the agency ought never to be confused with programs which, like those of HEW, deal in subsidies, contract themselves to other bureaucracies, and make awards under constant pressure from constituency lobbies. Nor did I want to see our awards determined in the same way as other social programs, by region, by population, by race or other factors. We needed a distinction that was fine but clear. I asked not that our funds *go* to the variously disadvantaged, but that we address their problems through the disciplines of learning:

> It is, perhaps, appropriate at this point, to affirm that at a time when the means whereby the social needs of the country are under careful review and indeed are being rethought in a fundamental way, the role of the humanities is paramount. For if the requirements of the young, the poor, the elderly, the ill, and the disadvantaged are to be addressed with justice and understanding, that effort must be guided by our best appreciation of the nature of man and society, and enlightened by the tradition of humanistic understanding.

It may be that this is lacking in piety. There is always a great deal of pressure to give money directly in order to redress social inequity. I thought that NEH would never have enough money for that, and that it might not be a question of money after all. I thought it better to persuade Congress that there were differing ways of looking at social programs. It would after all have been easy to make NEH a conduit of federal funds, to act in some respects as the Arts Endowment did, and distribute its funds among minorities, among the disadvantaged, among every kind of constituency with a claim to redress. That would have been a very short-run solution, allowing for popularity without accomplishment.

There were points of administration doctrine with which I agreed, and others that didn't make a great deal of sense to me. I didn't want to get into a war of doctrines and ideology. I was known as a man who could do business with Congress, not as a proponent of Executive power. I thought then, and still do, that this makes a lot of sense: government is a compromise. At any rate, at least in this case maneuver was the right tactic. The idea took hold that there was more than one form of social action, evidence (if not incontrovertible) that the policy worked.

The plans evolved for the use of Bicentennial funds called for an enormous number of new ideas. *The Adams Family Chronicle* was made possible only by the development of programming for public television, a development that took place within NEH as well as the Public Broadcasting System. The first step was acquisition or rental; it was astonishingly cheap to lease materials from the BBC and other sources until our own system of production could begin. But even putting BBC materials into some kind of sequence was at first fairly clumsy. American television has for a long time been divided between education and entertainment; providing a choice only between death by boredom and death by pelting with marshmallows. The scholars called upon to interpret humanities on television had not much idea of dealing with its audience. On the other hand, the networks were impatient with anything that got in the way of the show.

Fortunately, there was the example of Kenneth Clark and Alistair Cooke, which influenced our ideas if not our performance. I don't think that the Humanities Film Forum ever attained their urbanity, but it was willing to learn. Each of the ten films first selected for this program was surrounded by introductions and commentary. There were certain assumptions: some were chosen because, like the Olivier *Richard III,* they literally translated texts of the humanities. Others, like *The Cranes Are Flying,* were there because it was generally accepted that film could be humanistic.

The tactical success of the grant was encouraging. Some of the pictures were both good and entertaining. The Nicol Williamson version of *Hamlet* and the Alec Guinness *Oliver Twist* were genuinely important interpretations of character. The audience was large, and easily and cheaply reached. But the general audience was not the one we had entirely in mind. The channels of public television and the media were powerfully affected. In fact the coverage we got by newspaper was unprecedented. Columnists for both the metropolitan press and their country cousins began with the belief that movies were an art form. Their general theory was that television needed only the infusion of money to raise its tone and that such money, preferably delivered by government, would eventually support the production of movie art—and those who make it. We could never make good that bonanza, and I hope that no Administration will.

The Film Forum was developed by the Endowment itself but another grant of comparable magnitude, Courses By Newspaper, came from outside the agency. The demographic shift may have been reducing the college population but was increasing the numbers of those whose adult interests now had room for education. These were people without degrees, literate, interested in ideas. They were still intellectually alive, accustomed to taking one or more newspapers and to being substantively disappointed. In some respects, they were more capable of dealing with education than their younger counterparts. They could not pursue a full-time education but the distribution of a daily could connect them to virtually any campus in the country.

Newspapers are cheap; they are delivered to the home; they can be read, unlike televised material, at convenience. They need not be addressed to a lowest common denominator. Each course of about twenty lectures was prepared by a group of scholars. They made few compromises because credit had to be given and the course had to measure up both to the expectations of the Appropriations Committee and of the institutions involved:

> Mrs. Hansen: What will your first series comprise?
>
> Mr. Berman: The first series is going to be of a general nature on historical, economic, and scientific developments in the United States. The lead writer will be an eminent sociologist, Daniel Bell, professor of sociology at Harvard University. He is going to be followed by Carl Degler, professor at Stanford University and James Bonner, professor of biology at California Institute of Technology and a professor from the London School of Economics.
>
> In every one of these lectures there is going to be the equivalent of part of a college course. We hope they will add up, as a matter of fact, to a college course that can be taken virtually free of charge by readers or subscribers to these newspapers.

It was not to be a correspondence course. Texts were worked up which were rather good, and lectures like those of Bell came through without condescension.

The best news had to do with the scale of the enterprise. Beginning with the original distributor, the Copley News Service, the course was eventually carried in some two hundred newspapers. Since the course did not compete with hard news for space it made out well against astrology columns, comic strips and afterthoughts. Space was free, which was important. And because of that, distribution was free as well.

Among the hundreds of newspapers eventually to subscribe to the project were the *Orange Coast Daily Pilot, Dover State News, Honolulu Advertiser, Baton Rouge State Times, Memphis Commercial Appeal*—as well as the *Boston Globe, Washington Star* and *New York Daily News.* Coverage of the grant was intense for a number of reasons: regional newspapers are motivated by any connection between the press and public service. The lectures of Courses By Newspapers were *de facto* proof that the aspirations of the media itself were justified.

I've mentioned these two grants because they were exemplary. They attempted to reach large audiences, to make the NEH presence felt in the media, hence in Congress itself and to translate the humanities into a form likely to gain public interest. NEH had for some time spoken of its mission among audiences and large public institutions; so far as Congress, the media, and ourselves were concerned it was time to make good on that claim.

The film and television program of the Endowment sought to triple from 1973 to 1974. It would become as large as the entire agency, or the vision of that agency, as it was conceived in the eye of its founders. The main reason for such a program was that only about two percent of commercial and sixteen percent of public television was devoted to programs that were remotely humanistic. Our Office of Planning and Analysis believed that a demand for educational television existed which was unlikely to be met by persent supply; that there were probably thirty million viewers in a potential educational audience; and that the cost of reaching them would be derisory.

The BBC had provided an example of the success of high-quality public broadcasting. It began to entertain—and sometimes to affect—the American viewing public from *The Forsyte Saga* on. By 1973 *The Six Wives of Henry VIII* was the latest BBC enterprise. Based on the costs of production, it would be difficult for NEH to do much about providing similar educational programming. But, the cost of acquisition or rental worked out to about 1 cent per viewer-hour.

The budget put the matter to Congress with some attempt at diplomacy, stating that, "the history of both commercial and public broadcasting in this country indicates that without sustained and consistent guidance, as well as substantial financial investment, by an organization whose particular interest and priorities concern the humanities, American film and television producers will never produce the kind of high-quality film series in history (or other humanities subject areas) which is now a standard part of British television." One reason for this was cost, another was the absence of ideas. The ferocious conflicts between local channels and the Corporation for Public Broadcasting, those engaged in by the Public Broadcasting System; and the day-to-day scramble for existence all made innovative programming unlikely. Television succeeds or believes it succeeds by imitation.

It ought to be noted that the use of the BBC did not mean, at least for NEH, simply an act of imitation. In fact, much as the *productions* of BBC were to be valued, its *structure* could not be recommended. The annual budget of the BBC in ratio to the annual budget of Great Britain is much higher than anything comparable in the United States. It is a large bureaucracy, and we seem not to need very much more of that. But perhaps the most important thing to ponder is that the BBC functions like a Ministry of Culture. What the United States needs least of all is the intervention into its culture by bureaucracies which not only fund but produce.

There is a certain amount of mythology about the BBC. It does not make shows of the same quality as *Upstairs, Downstairs* across the board. It tries to put out a lot of programs on a little money. Quality necessarily varies tremendously. For every program that makes it big in the United States or in other markets there are many others not good enough to attract customers. There is in fact a certain resemblance to our own system of public broadcasting which is consantly tempted to put out less program on less money.

Typically, the BBC show has something to do with history, which allows it to take advantage of our nostalgia for a better past—and to utilize the costumes, sets and locations that lie so close at hand. But its technology is uninventive, its direction often stodgy, and little else up to the quality of its actors. It may be that the adaptation of novels will run its course.

What the BBC can offer as a model for us is the training and encouragement of talent, its interest in high culture or at least its refusal to abandon that, and the independence of its producers. We ought to realize that there has been a stunning absence of writers and critics from the deliberations of CPB and of PBS. We have, however, felt the topheavy presence of those whose political gravity assures membership; and of those who gather grapes in the government vineyards.

NEH had two responsibilities to fill in terms of program support: one, purely financial, was to make acquisition within its budget. Nothing mattered so much to our congressional committees as the assurance that all could be done within the stipulated limites. And, of course, *an entire series could be paid for at the same rate as one or two minutes of commercial advertisement,* a figure which pleased Congress enormously and which was almost continuously alluded to by our supporters in the House and the Senate—and by me. For half a million dollars we could put together a sequence of ten films, one showing per week. This carried with it the right to one or more re-runs. Since the rates of exchange were then favorable this responsibility was not hard to fulfill.

The second responsibility was imposed upon the agency. Success in programming meant that NEH inherited a new set of constituents. These constituents naturally enough wanted funding for public television to come from the federal government. They wanted funding to cover not only programming but operating expenses: and they were abetted by their house press and by columnists who argued for the federal support of public television.

It began to be expected, however, that the agency would not only acquire programs cheaply but produce them expensively. The object of constituents, and of media like *The Washington Post,* was in fact to imitate the BBC: to support cadres of actors, writers and producers,; to pay for air time; to underwrite the costs of national broadcasting culture. There was a great difference between assisting public television and subsidizing it. We did not want it or the media to transcend their gratitude.

Yet the pressure exerted for production and for its full support was inexorable. Actor's Equity and the AFL-CIO resented mere acquistion because very little of the money went to American sources. It was at one point convenient to apologize for this by noting that NEH paid TIME-LIFE and other intermediaries enough to make it worthwhile for their profits. The public made few critical distinctions. All in all, when the question of American production, support, and profit was raised, the response was unanimously in favor of government, which is to say NEH support of the whole enterprise. At this point we were forewarned that acquisition might be economical, but that we had created a constituency with appetites larger than such small morsels could satisfy.

There were certain resemblances between film and museum exhibition programs. Both dealt with audiences to be numbered in the millions. Both developed constituencies whose fundamental desire was for subsidy. Both brought the Endowment up against those who would once have been patrons of the arts or of culture in general; who now had become aware that the Federal government might relieve them of the cost of patronage while taking little from its influence. And both enterprises required a separation of territorial rights.

Senator Bible's remarks on museums addressed the last of these issues:

> How do you avoid overlapping the museum field with our good friend, Nancy Hanks? She came up with a museum program, and I think your predecessor—who was a professor from Rhode Island, Barnaby Keeney—I think he was the first one that grappled with this problem, and figured, by gosh, this is a place to get a few dollars more. . . . But how do you avoid overlap? There are so many instances of overlapping in this vast bureaucracy that we go to bed some nights and just can't sleep because we are worried about it.

The NEH museum program, like its film program, aimed to triple its budget, and to expend millions of dollars. But with that increase, and the natural competitiveness of the two agencies, came a territorial imperative.

The expansion of NEH coincided with the transformation of American museums. There are many more of them—over five thousand—than one expects. They cover science, fine arts, history, technology, medicine, and many other subjects. They are connected to other institutions, from the smallest historical associations to the largest universities. They draw visitors by the hundred million, the American Association of Museums pointing out that for several years now there have been more people attending exhibitions than football games. But there are liabilities as well. It costs a great deal to mount exhibitions; and it is sometimes impossible even to store holdings adequately. Private philanthropy can no longer support what was a phenomenon of public service. There has in short been a radical shift in costs, patronage, and the nature of the enterprise.

Before the boom in museum attendance, admission had customarily been free. Museums had been fairly secure financially, supported by community and individual activity. But philanthropy has changed with the times, most donors being extremely reluctant to underwrite what are essentially the costs of operation. Heating, air-conditioning, and simple maintenance are not as attractive as other kinds of public benefaction; nor are they as visible. Like the great research libraries, museums were by the mid-seventies curtailing their services. They closed off galleries, resisted traveling exhibits, and cut off many services (including security) that for a long time had been thought to be either natural or indispensable.

The administration of museums was rarely at its best. The explosion of costs and public service would on their own have taxed modern administrative capabilities. Most museums were ill-equipped to cut costs or develop new sources of support. In addition, they were in many cases unable to decide whether they should in fact function in an expanded public mode. Without being unncessarily critical, it should be said that museums have what amounts to a tradition of weak management. There are deep divisions between trustees, curators, and administrators. And the last simply do not have the training it takes to run an institution. Their abilities are for the most part diplomatic, which is to say that they have been accustomed to doing what other people want. By far the greatest difficulties NEH had in dealing with museums was in identifying what might or should be done, establishing a clear-cut way of doing it, and applying resolution to any kind of decision.

Caught with insufficient funds, in inflationary times, with no cadre of management able to cope with either money or policy matters, museums found themselves hopelessly behindhand. They were now centers for the community as well as of scholarship. Their collections were not so much *objets d'art* as part of public visual and historical consciousness. That implied certain functions for NEH: to keep up the scholarship of these institutions; to support their educational activities; and to assist their public programs, essentially interpretative exhibition.

The disciplines of the humanities do public service, but without an audience. Although there is every reason to expect that the work of the mind should take place in private, there seemed to be no reason why that work should not have a public presence. The example of the sciences was pretty straightforward: the mode of scientific research, validated by foundations, consulted by government, and influential in universities should have been *in some respects* central to the humanities. Granted the very great differences between science and humanities, there were still ends in common. The humanities needed but did not have a conception of humanistic education. While every scientist had a defined prejudice as to what students must know in order to graduate, humanists could not even agree whether the knowledge of a foreign language was essential. Scientists had strong professional associations; those involving the humanities simply proclaimed common interest in certain fields. Science had powerfully affected secondary education; the humanities responded to its deficiences. In short, the sciences were professional in a way the humanities were not, especially in their conception of what they did and how it was done.

Comparison between the two may be as unfair as their competition. The sciences were able to accomplish more because they had more money (about seventeen billion a year from all private and public sources) and more resources. But they had also a different idea about themselves. What they performed was not subject to instant re-definition; chemists did not proclaim the inutility of their experiements and physicians were not aliented from their own practice. Science, to use its favorite word, "advanced" with predictable regularity. If the humanities were to have self-confidence enough to "advance" as well, they needed institutions to help that. Almost three million dollars was being requested to pay for such institutions; really to create them. The hearings before the House indicate their programmatic form:

> Mrs. Hansen: You are requesting $2,700,000 for "Humanities Institutes." What does this involve?
>
> Mr. Berman: This is a new program that we have very high hopes for. One of the characteristics of American education for the past 10 or 15 years has been the establishment of places like the Center for Advanced Study in the Behaviorial Sciences at Stanford, the Institute for Advanced Studies—which really means mathematics, sociology and physics—at Princeton, a whole variety of institutes throughout the United States that in the most incredibly lopsided way favors the non-humanistic disciplines. It has not been possible for any American humanist [to study within adequate facilities] . . . matters of the first importance to the humanities.

Until Roger Rosenblatt (now of *TIME* magazine) took over and transformed the NEH Division of Education Programs, the theory and practice of these institutes were to lack leadership. But even at this time it could be seen that La Jolla, Palo Alto, and Princeton held examples for their poor relations.

At this stage, planning for the support of institutes before they existed, we could see only so far ahead. Regardless of the special purposes of any of these places, they had certain common features to define. Institutes have traditionally been centers of research, and that was to be a major function. But they also had to provide professional and national services; the first in the training of postgraduate faculty and the second in relation to the small colleges scattered everywhere that rely on the centers of thought. There are over three thousand institutions of higher learning in this country, most of which have too few books, and too litle money and training, to accomplish their own purposes. If institutes were able to affect the rank and file of education they could accomplish even more than their scientific counterparts. Tactics later devised by Roger Rosenblatt were aimed at this, such as committing the small institutions which had sent their best hopes to an NEH institute at Yale or Chicago to making a place in their curriculum for the work and ideas brought back home.

How useful could such institutes hope to be? With the money available in the foreseeable future we might be able to afford three of these multi-million dollar structures. They would be able to circulate about thirty national fellows a year through each, and to run programs involving more people than that regionally. The enterprise was a middle ground; its numbers not meaning much when compared to the quarter-million teachers of humanities in this country but mattering a good deal when measured by the force of its example. The teaching of humanities is supersensitive to style, and to the hierarchy of status which demarcates individuals and institutions. Example matters more for it than it does for other professions. The problem would not be numbers, especially considering the multiplier effect these institutes were designed to have, taking programs from centers of scholarship and transplanting them to other places. The real issues would be the degree to which the great universities would support the projects—and their success in making institutes meaningful. We had provided only money and structure, the rest was up to them.

At the other end of the academic spectrum was the largest and most difficult of all bodies to affect: millions of students enrolled in thousands of humanities courses throughout the country. I didn't believe that there was much to be done for them. I had no use for programs that would remain purely symbolic. I did not think that undergraduates could handle grants. I feared that the ideology of youth and its sentimentality would color anything that was accomplished. I loathed the whole idea. The staff of the Office of Planning and Analysis, led by Armen Tashdinian, loved it.They were right and I was wrong. The Youthgrants in the Humanities that evolved were good in a variety of ways and some of the work that resulted was of real public interest.

The procedure began by assembling panels of men and women—I should say boys and girls—ranging from about sixteen to about twenty-six. There were a good many undergraduates. But the panels were probably better than many run by scholars experienced in committees and confirmed in the ways of foundations. I sat in on a number of them, and was much amused by the deflation of my prejudice. The questions asked by the panel about applications were sharp and even brutal; they were too impatient to be devious. They knew about work on their own level from the inside and were not confused by adult preconceptions. They were also very stingy. And compared to their feelings about the posturing of youth, my own opinions seemed nothing less than romantic. These young panelists were not emotionally or intellectually ungenerous. The staff that chose them would have been, if there were such a possibility, Democratic Socialists. The colleges they came from represented academic life across the board. There were a high density of minorities. The panelists were nominated by federal and other organizations that had youth-related programs. They were, in short, pretty much what they seemed to be, a generation of the 'seventies, with its own values about intellectual work and its quality. Sometimes a thoughtless comparison is made between the young generations of the 'sixties and the 'seventies, with nostalgic praise lavished on the "commitment" of the former. The latter seemed pretty good to me.

The program itself was a bureaucrat's dream, a model of checks, balances, and obstacles. In that respect it typified agency policy which was thorough to the point of relentlessness. The guidelines emphasized the humanities. We did not expect youthgrants to be concerned with professional research, but it was hoped that they would look at social and other issues through particular disciplines. And in fact applicants as well as panelists were required by the guidelines to make a distinction:

> Because the Endowment is charged with developing the humanities as sources of insight into contemporary human problems, it is sometimes thought to be concerned with "social action." In the very immediate sense it is not. Social action and humanities disciplines such as philosophy, jurisprudence, ethics may investigate the same existing situation but they do so with different motives: the humanities seek initially to understand; social action, to change. Endowment-supported projects, therefore, are directed at comprehension rather than change.

It is possible that these may be thought to be fighting words. But they live up to the law and my own intentions, which were Erasmian.

The criteria for award tried to impose whatever structure could be borne. I would have liked to emulate scientific precision, but that can't be done for many things in the humanities. What could be asked was that projects use and develop knowledge, that they display a sense of method, and that they be of some use to the grantee, if not to the rest of us.

Some of the projects were quite splendid. We had initially wondered whether we might not be unleashing squadrons of adolescents armed with tape recorders upon the unsuspecting aged. Oral history has for a while been popular because it doesn't take much talent and people do like to talk. There were in fact oral history projects in both Youthgrants and regular professional research. When done well there is a lot that can be learned from those who recall the life they led in a different kind of country. If we consider the change in black national life since the Second World War it can be seen that some lives are historical resources. But most Youthgrant projects went beyond this, into the study of language, archaeology and many other disciplines. There was even a minor triumph: the President expressed an interest in a Tammany politician who had caught the eye of Churchill just at the time that a twenty-year old grantee discovered, as part of his NEH project, whole boxes and files full of his memoirs.

The Division of Research would normally be less visible than its counterparts in the Endowment. But there were two reasons for much wider interest in its work, the first that it administered the New York Public Library grant, the second that the Bicentennial had made the study of American history and institutions genuinely interesting to Congress, the media, and the public.

I suppose that pound for pound this division ran the most expensive of our projects. It was the one dearest to the heart of the American Council of Learned Societies, and of nearly all other scholarly associations. There had been a tremendous loss of research funds from other sources. Universities in the seventies had to cut their losses. They could no longer afford to finance projects, provide overhead expenses, or even to publish what they once might have considered to be material indispensable to their interests. Foundations are not especially interested in scholarly research that is slow, quiet, and not apt to pay an immediate social dividend. And there was of course the example of the Ford Foundation, which made the momentous decision to abolish its program of assistance to the humanities. In part this was a reaction to the new role of government and in part a decision to support other social goods, notably the performing arts.

Research projects at the Endowment were complex and expensive; they involved enormous masses of material that could be handled only by groups of investigators. Because salaries and benefits had to be paid for these groups, with their attendant staff and office expenses, and because of high overhead and other costs, research had not done well at NEH before the expansion of the agency. Ironically, Richard Nixon's decision to support our extrapolated growth benefitted those most opposed to him. Most academics were quite aware of this—and, sometimes, gave credit where it was due.

It was no less ironic that the general intellectual mood had made support of research difficult. There was so much pressure to address "problems," to unleash the humanities upon the inequities of life, to tie their funds to good causes, that ordinary, basic research seemed socially unjustified. The budget defense in fact admitted what had long been argued by those who had once lobbied for the agency's creation:

> The funding of research grants has been deliberately kept at low levels during the past five years in order to concentrate the limited appropriations available on other program areas considered most pressing. The need to redress within colleges and universities the imbalance resulting from heavy Federal investment in the sciences and the need to create a basic program capability in the public sector, where there had been none, has required NEH to devote the major part of new funds to areas served by the Education and Public programs, leaving insufficient funds for research. Thus applications for research were discouraged either directly by Endowment staff or indirectly as the Endowment's priorities became known to the scholarly community.

The situation reads like the script for *La Ronde:* the academy successfully diffuses the idea that government is responsible for all forms of social welfare. Congress, which sometimes has a weakness for ideas, urges a miniature agency devoted among other things to archeology, linguistics, and the criticism of poetry to do something about national problems. The Council of that agency responds by agreeing to spend its funds on cities, civil rights, the environment, and "war, peace and foreign policy." The staff is happy to comply, inasmuch as these things get more attention from the world. And the academy, which has originally lobbied for the agency, is enraged by the discovery that its funds will not go for their designated purposes—until the advent of Richard Nixon! The news that the largest increase in the NEH budget would go to the Division of Research—from the previous level of three million to the new level of ten million dollars—caused an enormous sigh of relief everywhere, and had, as money does, a very conciliating effect.

The idea behind the new budget for Research was not so much to entertain new projects as to allow for more structural and institutional strength. In addition to the normal run of applications we hoped to specialize, and to concentrate resources. There were to be programs now for editing and for centers of research; for the production of complex materials like bibliographies, atlases, dictionaries, and encyclopedias; for conferences and for development of state histories.

The Division of Research had three successive heads from 1972–1977. William Emerson was followed by Simone Reagor and Harold Cannon. From the New York Public Library grant to the programs for editing and for research institutes, they left their mark upon their division. They managed also to preserve continuity, one of the best examples of which concerns the papers left by the Founding Fathers of this country.

The superb biography of Thomas Jefferson by Dumas Malone has taken a lifetime of scholarship. It has been one of the great NEH projects, supported for many years in a style worth its accomplishment. It is an example of more than scholarship, because Jefferson has long been a central figure to the Endowment. Before the Bicentennial was really much pondered, the Endowment had tried to see itself, and have the world see it, in Jeffersonian terms. The Malone life is necessarily one of the central things for the agency because of its extraordinary quality of analysis; because it exemplifies the agency's interest in the lives, journals and works of the Founding Fathers; and because it expresses so completely the beliefs of Thomas Jefferson. It may have been first a grant, but it became our totem.

I think that in order to explain the importance of editing we have to understand the life and work behind that task. In the case of Jefferson we see (not often in American life) a sense of equilibrium between public and private purposes. Knowledge mattered to Jefferson, and the importance of his example, at least for NEH, was the way he combined humanistic with pragmatic learning. The inventor of the moldboard plough was, for example, able to read Homer in Greek and knew a great amount of Milton. He recommended the study of poetry to the young and himself read, as Malone puts it, "more for profit than pleasure." He knew Shakespeare and the foreign languages, the Bible and a rather large amount of philosophy. There is a passage in Malone's first volume that sums up what learning meant to Jefferson:

> His appetite never ceased to be Gargantuan but even he had to make some selection; and he did this, not in the fastidious spirit of a *gourmet,* but in the mood of an ambitious workman who wanted to build up his strength. He greatly desired to make of himself a cultivated person, he did not scorn the traditional embellishments of genteel life, and he loved learning and the arts for their own sake. But, as one who lived in a new and undeveloped country, he was most anxious to acquire knowledge that was useful to man. He regarded the human mind, not as a toy to be played with, but as an instrument to be used in the cause of progress.

If it was good enough for Jefferson, it was good enough for me.

This grant conveyed something of the excitement of intellectual life, and of the pleasures that can be sometimes found in duty. It was the flagship of the editing program, which supported work on Washington, Jay, Webster, and others. These books are exciting and important. The life of Booker T. Washington sponsored by the Endowment is not simply a monument to scholarship. It is one of the things without which modern life cannot be understood. If the knowledge of basic research should be put off; and if the balance between "useful" and "pure" learning should be impatiently destroyed by some administration intent on mailing out money for votes, the spirit of Jefferson would haunt our incomplete lives.

CHAPTER VI

The Limits of Authorization

I have so far talked about congressional appropriations, those funds which are given to any agency annually and constitute its budget. One must work almost continuously with appropriations committees because preparation for hearings for one year begin almost as soon as those for the preceding year have ended. And agencies of any size, even NEH, maintain a full-time staff whose purpose is to appear in congressional offices any day of the week, chat up their opposite numbers, and lubricate the great machine. In addition, every agency undergoes authorization or the re-writing of its enabling legislation. In our case, that took place every three years. Authorization extends the life of the agency for whatever period Congress wishes, sets the theoretical limits for its expenditures (of which annual appropriations may be any fraction pleasing Congress) and either liberates the agency or penalizes it by including in the law any of an infinite number of injunctions or codicils. For example, the authorization committee was pleased with the American Film Institute, a grantee of the Arts Endowment, so it simply wrote in the 1973 amendment to Public Law 89–209 that a certain portion of the annual budget of NEA would be devoted to AFI. That meant that this favorite institution would more or less automatically and without application receive several million dollars each year.

Authorization hearings began in 1973 with hearings for the two cultural agencies before a joint committee headed by John Brademas of the House Committee on Education and Labor and Claiborne Pell of the Senate Committee on Labor, Public Welfare and Education. The members of Congress displayed considerable annoyance with the Administration, tempered by sympathy for the two Endowments. The question endlessly arose why we should be so fortunate as to increase and multiply our budgets while all other domestic agencies were in want. I was by now geting used to taking bread from the mouths of orphans, and outlined some reasons why the support of humanities might be interpreted as a social enterprise. I was fairly successful with that but less successful at establishing in the minds of the members that our great responsibility was to our professional programs. Senator Pell especially was dissatisfied with the proportion of awards—most of them going to the academic profession—and asked that five percent of the budget be set aside for those without college degrees. I had previously reminded him that the Humanities Endowment resembled the National Science Foundation more than it did the Arts Endowment which is to say that it dealt with established disciplines and professions. Our awards were not a matter of *style* but were based on competition between those whose merits could reasonably be evaluated. The chances of someone without a B.A. getting a fellowship, in a competition which included the entire faculties of Berkeley, Chicago or Yale, were just about nil. I added now that our new public programs, especially in film and museums, took care of the general public automatically. They were, after all, the beneficiaries of such programs, and shared the Endowment's money with professionals. The only difference was that they received their benefits *en masse*.

John Brademas observed that the Bicentennial was something of a scandal, then took the position that the current success of the two agencies persuaded him we could do better with funds for the national celebration than any conceivable alternate agencies. Other members of the two committees made their opinions felt; and since this was an occasion that took place only every few years, as compared to he annual grinding of gears in appropriations, there was a good deal of discussion on the broad ends of the Endowment. Members of both Houses were friendly but not intensively interested in the disciplines which they had originally chartered. By far the most questions were addressed to political matters: what we did for the young or for those without degrees; how we situated ourselves in an administration hostile to Congress and already in the throes of Watergate; what we were going to *do* for the public. The most important question, which was to affect the later character of the agency and cause my resignation, derived from the congressional appetite for direct public benefits.

The members of the Senate wanted the Endowment to relate its work directly to their constituencies. Senator Javits of New York, for example, urged that members of the AFL-CIO be placed on the National Council for the Arts. Senator Bentsen of Texas wanted NEH money to go directly to state bureaucracies. Senator Pell of Rhode Island wanted NEH to act exactly like NEA, that is, to give a quota of twenty percent of its funds annually to such groups. This time, the Committee could be held off. The Endowment had, after all, managed to create a State-Based program which combined public and humanistic ends. It already supported regional activities.

At this point a brief review might be helpful. Our state committees were formed of volunteer groups who received a single block grant each year from the Endowment. In turn, they gave out many small grants to local applicants. They were encouraged to give such grants to local historical societies, campuses and libraries. And these grants paid for many forums on debateable issues. We hoped that our congressional overseers would be satisfied to find significant amounts of money devoted to regional causes. And, that they would respect the composition of these groups. The committee for Rhode Island, for example, was typical in having the president of the state university, a justice of the Superior Court, a newspaper editor, various professors from different places and disciplines, and a variety of members from the general public, including representatives of unions, business, civic and minority organizations.

The committees began with small amounts of money, then got enough (eventually more than half a million dollars a year each) to make congressional interest grow. There were restrains on these committees, indispensable because the desire of Congress to send money back home through this particlar viaduct was in no special way connected to our function. I required the committees to be perceptibly concerned with the humanities; to involve college faculty in their operation; to give their annual benefactions around a given plan rather than at random; and to recognize the overall authority of the agency. For something with all these conflicting motives it worked surprisingly well; these Pushme-Pullyou committees raised a good deal of matching money from their localities and tried hard to do things which actually were humanistic.

I did not want these committees to become independent of our power and dependent on our financing. To give them a quota of our annual funds would be to remove those funds from their designated use. It would set up fifty bureaucracies, all rivals of NEH and of each other. And it would have one effect opposite to that desired: it would benefit state government, which itself could be decidedly monolithic. Senator Javits accepted my arguments, and there was a compromise. It was at least temporarily recognized that NEH was very different from its sister agency. We did not subsidize. We did not act as a conduit for unstoppable Federal benefits. Our committees were not appointed by the governments of each state: they were groups of volunteers from the academic profession and the concerned public. No new language seemed called for in the bill, and we were free until 1976.

After the committee hearings, the authorization bill for the two Endowments came to the floor of both Houses. Debate began in the House of Representatives with—could it have been otherwise?—the opposition to the committee report of H. R. Gross of Iowa. Gross was the traditional enemy of the Endowments: a lifetime spent in the House defending the integrity of savings had culminated in ten years of happy hostility to culture. He was the burglar alarm of the Congress. Not a bad man to have in government, but something of an inconvenience. He was dangerous to the extent that he might serve as a focus for more able opposition.

Certain distinctions were transparently symbolic. Gross was old, narrowly midwestern, and Republican. His chief adversary, John Brademas, was young, cosmopolitan, and Democratic. One fought his own party, the other helped the enemy:

Mrs. Brademas. Mr. Speaker, the bill originated with a legislative proposal by President Nixon, as well as by bills introduced by Members of the House, both Democrats and Republicans, as well as in the other body.

Mr. Gross. And it came out of the committee of which the gentleman is a member?

Mr. Brademas. I am delighted to say that it was reported favorably by the subcommittee which I have the honor to chair, without a single dissenting vote from either the majority or minority members, and it won such widespread support of the full Committee on Education and Labor that it was approved by a voice vote.

Mr. Gross. So it is pretty clear the gentleman is on the same wavelength as the administration.

Mr. Brademas. I am delighted to say for the first time this year I find myself enthusiastically on the same wavelength as the administration.

The defense of the authorization bill was pitched almost exclusively on political grounds. The Arts Endowment was understood to be a kind of domestic program whose mission it was to disseminate "experience" to inner cities and rural areas rather than create works of art. Frank Thompson of New Jersey, one of the original sponsors of arts and humanities legislation, argued that the function of the Arts Endowment could be defined by the services it provided for a national audience: especially for ghettos, farm communities, schools, and local organizations. Many more services were discussed and, as might be expected, the examples of art patronage in the ancient world and in the Renaissance were frequently brought in. But there was something of a difference, since what we know about patronage in the past suggests that the creation of art was its object. In this case, the social services that art might confer were being confused with its main object. Art was now understood to be a sequence of performances.

Here are two especially revelatory passages about the politics of constituency and numbers:

> Decentralization of the arts activity is not only bringing art into remote and disadvantaged areas of the country, it is also generating the flow of creative art forms coming out of such areas. Folk music and crafts of all kinds, springing from proud regional or ethnic tradition deep in our Nation's history, are being rediscovered, brought back into the life of our communities, and preserved for future generations. The cultural traditions of Appalachia, the American Indian, Black Americans, Spanish-speaking communities, and the host of national and ethnic groups which have made up our great country, are a part of the agenda for the NEA.

This statement, subscribed to by Julia Hansen, John Brademas, Albert Quie and Marvin Esch, is the quintessence of a new definition of art. I have taken this up in detail in a later chapter; at this point I will say only that the sense of what art does is fairly populistic, even though new social groups are being addressed.

The second passage is informative in a different way. The speaker is Wiley Mayne of Iowa:

> Iowa has one of the greatest percentages of population aged 65 or older. It is therefore particularly fitting that the Iowa Arts Council this year provided assistance to the Iowa State Commission on the Aging for a senior citizen arts festival, an event which proved highly successful and which I hope will be repeated yearly. We have an immense reservoir of training, experience, and talent in older Americans—upon retirement they have increased time to devote to these talents, to their crafts and hobbies. The Federal, State and local programs in the arts should take particular cognizance of their needs and their potentialities.

This is a fairly naked plea to fund hobbies for the retired. If congressional expectations were to prevail, then both endowments would almost certainly become conduits of funds to special interest groups. In my opinion, NEA was already on that slippery slope—and willingly. One reason for its fantastically good relationship with Congress was that it did what Congress wanted it to do.

But there were other passages I had in mind, among them that of Tocqueville:

> When none but the wealthy had watches, they were almost all very good ones: few are now made which are worth much, but everyone has one in his pocket. . . . Not that, in democracies, the arts are incapable, in case of need, of producing wonders. . . . But they have rarely an opportunity of showing what they can do; they are scrupulously sparing of their powers; they remain in a state of accomplished mediocrity. . . . In aristocracies, a few great pictures are produced; in democratic countries, a vast number of insignificant ones.

Tocqueville describes a natural course of events. Possibly his ideas can be extended, and we can surmise that education in, say, literature, will follow the path of those watches and paintings he has in mind. I believe, actually, that that will happen: in the near future the nation will in a rudimentary way be literate with computers and in a curtailed language of general expressiveness, and pretty much unfamiliar either with the books or the art that are usually thought to be basic to our character and values.

At any rate, the bill passed in spite of opposition. H. R. Gross had already given one reason for opposition, that of fiscal responsibility. It was generally rejected on the grounds that no matter how much the two agencies grew they could not begin to affect the total federal budget. He then tried criticism of some NEH grants (he often managed to confuse these, intentionally, with those given by the Smithsonian which dealt with the sex life of cockroaches or other suitably outrageous subjects) and only blundered into errors of fact and style. He had support from Edith Green, Jack Kemp and Phil Crane, but they were disorganized and had few compelling arguments. Crane came closest to a unified field theory of opposition to cultural support when he invoked Michael Harrington's critique of "the congressional practice of creating programs that represent socialism for the rich and free enterprise for the poor." But no one in the House followed him up.

Senator Proxmire did a better job than his counterparts in attacking the two agencies. He spent some time developing the point that arts subsidies benefited those who might otherwise have made up deficits from private sources. He did chase a number of red herrings, among them the idea that the federal government might eventually censor or control culture. Nancy Hanks and I had long since learned, however, that the social tides capable of moving the congressional fleet could capsize our little boats. We did not know whether it was more amusing to be accused of tyranny, or to consider how little capable we were of inflicting it. We also know that it was much easier for the constituency to influence the agency than the other way around.

With the end of congressional debate a number of points had been made aside from the resultant legislation. There was some handwriting on the wall for NEH: congressional expectations in general were that public benefits would be provided to every category of constituent. And in particular, both House and Senate wanted a State-Based program which would absorb federal money without too much logic-chopping as to what it might accomplish. The Congress liked turnstile figures, big events, and big audiences. It was fond of programs that could be linked however adventitiously to social problems: if legislation on assistance to the cities or to the handicapped was stalled, then Arts and Humanities offered a symbolic opportunity to go on record for good causes. The idea was to give as much money as possible to as many people as possible—especially those organized in blocs, groups, associations or in other politically conscious ways.

CHAPTER VII

The Criticism of Growth

Opposition to our growth having petered out, it now remained to deal with critics and constituents.In June, 1974, William F. Buckley, Jr. asked me to appear on "Firing Line" to answer what were plainly some difficult questions. We were good friends, and still are, but I expected nothing less than what he would deliver, which was an open and intelligent attack on cultural support.

By now I was something of a problem to conservatives. They were pleased by the idea of good government and wished me personal success. But the trouble was, this little agency had grown so much under my Machiavellian hand that it was now part and parcel of big government. Conservative thought about government springs from the logic of minimal intervention. Government does have legitimate functions, among them national defense, but otherwise should keep its hands off things better done by the private sector. In the case of culture, insult was added to injury, for those who benefit from the patronage of government tend to be liberal technocrats already convinced that wealth should be redistributed through taxation. And, in subsidizing culture, government affects it, managing at the same time to reduce taxation revenue while debasing ideas. The argument makes sense, particularly if it is confined to the writing of constitutions. But what if government already exists in a form not easily changed? There are billions of dollars involved, and thousands of jobs, not to speak of the inertia of decades. There is no changing of structures or stopping activities without legislation; and this means a new kind of adversary relationship between the institutions of government itself. It has taken about half a century to expand modern federal government and it may take a good deal of time to deflate it.

Bill Buckley did an excellent job of bringing conservative theory to bear, and I did what I could to suggest that government—or at least my Monaco-sized piece of it—could be defended. We began with two basic issues: whether high culture could compete on the free market, and whether private philanthropy was enough to help it out. Neither of us got into the even more fundamental issue of whether or not high culture should be judged by its success in the free market. That is the view of libertarianism; and I thought it roughly equivalent to the ancient practice of infant exposure. We both agreed that there was such a thing as a "public good" excempt from the usual procedures of the marketplace.

Before expressing some differences we had one further agreement: that inflation itself was not a final argument for government support of art or the humanities. We knew that we had to go deeper than that, to inquire really if there has been a significant cultural change since America first developed its great public institutions. To my mind there had been such a change: our museums were now essentially public services undertaken at a tremendous loss. They were ready now to change from one kind of public service to another. They drew astonishing audiences. They mounted extraordinary exhibitions. They negotiated with foreign governments. In short, they played an important role in national cultural life. The Metropolitan Museum of Art was no more local than its great contemporary down Fifth Avenue, the New York Public Library. Both had become national institutions, and both represented the change that had occurred in many of our universities, museums, libraries, and research centers.

Buckley said that he could be persuaded we had a function if the case could be made that great ability otherwise unrecognized were to be sustained by government. I had to answer, much to my sorrow, that this was unlikely. The reason was paradoxical: not that we had poor cultural vision but that it is unlikely for anyone sufficiently earnest ever to go with his beak unfilled. The United States is knee-deep in artistic intentions, and rare is the man without his grant, even for extending dry wash across the Colorado River. NEH could not apologize for failing to discover merit; it could only sustain disinterested judgment. But sometimes tactics become strategy: our system of review was rigorous and it made the case for competitive merit. We were a single-purpose organization, with professional expertise. We differed from private foundations in being more accountable.

The Endowment could not apologize for being part of the federal government, nor for being implicated in the mysteries of tax deduction. The view that government is excessive seems true enough, but the part of that excess devoted to humanities (about one four-thousandth of the federal budget) suggested that we were a target of opportunity. Perhaps criticism should direct itself at more significant or more outrageous amounts of money. As for the tax code, there was no doubt about the strange marriage of philanthropy and deduction. Anyone who gave gifts to NEH could declare the amount when he filed his taxes. Yet, the six-million dollar grant to the New York Public Library had in it only two million taken from the Treasury. The rest were matching funds; and anyone with philosophical objections to the matter might first wish to count slowly up to four million.

My business wasn't the decision of IRS to allow deductions for gifts to cultural institutions; it was only to get enough money from the private sector to convince Congress that the cost was being shared.

I speculated about one other point in the concluding debate with the audience: NEH was in some ways the equivalent of a large private foundation. But it was put together by taxpayers as if it were a huge mutual fund, giving them or their representatives the power of patronage traditionally reserved for wealth. I don't know how compelling that is, nor how the situation will change with the times. Eventually taxpayers may feel that Arts and Humanities the way they feel about government in general. The hidden assumption of the debate was that what I did was theoretically suspect, and could only be justified by how well I did it. Or, as I have put the matter to Members of Congress after resignation, the issue is managerial and not legislative. It is the Chairman's interpretation of the law that makes him worthy of praise or blame.

Almost immediately after this public defense of the agency's function the process of appropriation began again, this time with some new variables. The chairmanship of the House subcommittee on appropriations would soon be vacant with the retirement of Julia Hansen. The new chairman would be either Sid Yates of Illinois of Gunn McKay of Utah, both at this point not really known to the agency. McKay was my fourth or fifth appointment in the rounds of the committee, and when I finally got to him I wasn't entirely sure it was a good idea. We had a pretty hostile talk about what the humanities did—very little—for the state of Utah. McKay was far from pleased by the media coverage of the New York Public Library grant which he saw as simply another conveyance of federal funds to the East. He was for economy, for the plains and mountain states, for popular benefits—and against most of what I had in mind. I nursed my wounds and went on to see everyone else on the list. There was a chilling interview with Ted Stevens of Alaska, who said accurately enough that we had few enemies in the Senate but not many friends.

I suppose the high point of these talks was getting to talk to Edith Green and George Mahon. The latter was chairman of the full House committee on appropriations, and an institution in his own right, with more than forty years in Congress. To talk to him was implicitly to have been taken seriously by the House. Edith Green was one of our old enemies who had joined in the amendments against our authorization, and done what she could to hold us down. I gave her what I hoped was one of the great salestalks of the Western world; and after a half-hour of eloquence staggered out of her office with the assurance that she might change her mind.

The hearings themselves began badly. The Arts were well roasted for their demographic quotas. Michael Straight skilfully and honestly defended the practice of giving funds to second-rate people and places, pointing out that they were after all in the majority. But the Members were pretty brutal, and witnesses from NEA generally talked to empty chairs while the committee made endless phone calls, got into private discussions, joked with each other and in every other way showed their amiable contempt, and the relationship of their powers to our own.

The Arts didn't really need to make a coherent argument, but we were dead in the water without one. So, whenever Julia asked a question, and then turned away to chat I quickly said something, then stopped as if I had given the answer. I looked complacent, and as she was fumbling with the next question I went into my spiel, which totally arrested the timing of the committee. The thing went along like a Marx Brothers chase for about fifteen minutes, and all we needed was Harpo beeping on his pogo stick. But things settled down, and I said my piece in detail.

The aim of NEA at hearings was to relate its work to the private interests of the committee, to induce belief in the enormous demand for money from the Arts, to talk of large constituencies satisfied, to speak of art as a common activity shared by voters and their families, to invoke connections between the abstractions of Art and youth, or Art and age, or Art and minorities. The aim of NEH was bound to be different, whether on principle or by necessity. It was absolutely essential for us to approach Congress in terms of achievements and costs. The two kinds of dialogues were radically different, one addressing itself to the popularity of *programs,* the other to the effect of *grants.*

I never allowed discussion to move far from the consideration of specific grants and their consequences. It made argument more manageable, but the real reason for this kind of concentration was that it provided a context. I could begin with the reason why, describe the action taken, and ask the committee to evaluate its meaning. In the case of the two grants now before the committee such consideration itself was a kind of success:

> Mr. Berman: I think that television can still be described in the words used about a decade ago: It is basically a vast wasteland.

Mrs. Hansen: A vast wasteland. It is worse than that most nights of the week.

Mr. Berman: I hope you have liked Tuesday nights when we have been able to put on *War and Peace.*

Mrs. Hansen: I have watched some of these.

Mr. McDade: I was privileged to watch most of the programs of *War and Peace,* and I think it is clearly one of the most outstanding things I have seen done on television. I think that mirrors as well many of the other things that the humanities has sponsored on television, that have helped tremendously to increase the quality in television programs in the United States. . . . We do handle the FCC in another committee. We constantly talk to them about the quality of television in the United States of America. It may be that the best way to achieve improvements in quality is to foster such programs as exemplified by *War and Peace.*

The ensuing discussion had more than one advantage: the Members shared with nearly every one else feelings ranging from disappointment to loathing; and they were deeply conscius of the waste of sums nearly congressional in magnitude by the networks. Our first extravaganza, the Humanities Film Forum, had cost about three cents per viewer: but *War and Peace* would reach even more people at a fraction the cost of that, perhaps three-quarters of a cent per viewer. A good many changes could be run on costs:

Mr. Berman: We participated with Mobil in *War and Peace;* they not only put up half the costs, but they paid for many of the things that helped its success including school study guides, brochures and advertisements.

Mr. Yates: How much did that cost?

> Mr. Berman: That cost the government roughly $275,000, which, as I have previously remarked, is the cost of about 1 minute of commercial time of the Super Bowl.

The grant solved three problems both for me and for the Committee: it cost little, changed a problem into a solution, and demonstrated that what was humanistic could also be public.

The mouse was still roaring—I suggested to the Committee that we might eventually compete with commercial television as well as raise public television out of its doldrums. In fact the association of NEH, the BBC and Mobil Oil was to have some historical effect: shows like *The Adams Family Chronicle* and *Roots* developed because of a new concept in programming, as well as a new sense of public capacities. The Endowment had not only struck a nerve in the body politic but managed, so to speak, to focus the irritation of Congress. In subsequent messages of the FCC and other government agencies, in discussion outside committee, and especially in response to constituents the arguments provided by NEH were diffused. It was a coincidental moment because public television had not fulfilled its promise and seemed now to be a natural connection to the humanities—if not a helpful dependent.

War and Peace cost about three-quarters of a cent per viewer on its first showing and only about a tenth of a cent per viewer the second time around. These were powerful arguments for a Congress that needed the reputation for economy. It was more important perhaps that the grant was not simply a *sucés d'estime.* It reached twenty million viewers and a small but influential body of critics. Although it had been acquired through the BBC the show transcended previous serializations; and we were not held responsible for its failing to be produced by Americans. As one writer put it, the show might have been made by MGM in the good old days, if MGM had had taste and literary understanding. The critical reception in general took the program to be a new start in public programming. It managed to translate Tolstoy into televised form because, dwarfing all previous efforts, including the six-hour Soviet version of Sergei Bondarchuk, it coped with the amplitude of the story. There were over fourteen hours of the series, every minute of which was needed. One of the results was a firm conception (renewed for both critics and audience) of *War and Peace* as a novel rather than an extended 1812 Symphony.

The tremendous density of *War and Peace* covers a domestic scene with all the interest of Dickens and Balzac; and the show brought out a powerful sense of nineteenth-century romance, as well as of social and family life. The words became as well known now as the music. After a while the critics dropped their pencils, and confessed simply that they were too interested in the oceanic flow of the story to do more than appreciate it, and wait for next week's show. I felt that way too, and though there clearly wasn't anything I could do for Tolstoy, it was nice to introduce him to new people.

Aside from the popularity of the grant one other thing mattered almost to the exclusion of all else: had it in fact translated the humanities from one form and one audience to another? Had my claim been made good that scholarship and public programs were compatible? I think the points were made by the acquisition of *War and Peace,* and made even more emphatically by another grant at the same time. In February, 1974, the Metropolitan Museum of Art put on a show with the rather low-key title *Masterpieces of Tapestry from the 14th to the 16th Centuries.* It was to become better known as the *Unicorn Tapestries,* an exhibition which broke the Metropolitan's attendance record, and which was part of the stunning sequence of international exhibitions from China, Russia, Egypt, and France.

The *Unicorn* began as a gleam in the eye of Thomas Hoving, Director of the Met. I abetted him—the two of us being, in the eyes of the museum establishment, something in the nature of unindicted co-conspirators. We were quite shameless in our desire for more and bigger international exhibitions. When we talked about this one it seemed like a rational attempt to uphold the reputation of both our institutions for scholarship;

and that an important part of medieval life would be presented to an appreciative but limited audience. When people began pouring into the Met by the thousand and the hundred thousand we began to get a different sense of what we had wrought.

For one thing, it turned out that middle-class taste was somewhat different from the view of it normally prevailing. And perhaps this held for middle-class perceptions as well. When the crowds began coming to this exhibition it struck me that there were new reasons for attendance. As most of our social institutions have declined, the sequence has gone from church to family to education; and with the loss of nerve and presence of mind of the latter, museums have become a replacement. Museums are in some respects the temples of the middle class. They arouse feelings once reserved for religion and the past; a powerful combination, and much more than nostalgia.

The rediscovery of the past, whether that implies the Renaissance or the nineteen-fifties has come about because the present is not satisfactory. I don't think that the interest in the past is a consequence of "identity" or "ethnicity" or other glozes upon time. Our interest lies in the fact that the world was once understood. The forgotten techniques of weaving in medieval Europe make history intelligible. When the viewer is in the present of the Unicorn tapestries he admits necessarily his ignorance of their religion, their courtly code, and their mystery of symbols. But the least educated of us becomes keenly aware that works of the past are intelligible. It is not that they are "realistic—after all, the symbology of the Unicorn is more vague to us than the meaning of a Picasso or a Pollack. The Unicorn tapestries have the effect upon us that the Greek vase had upon Keats—and that the work of Piero della Francesca had upon Berenson. They comfort the eye by harmonies which may not be fully understood.

The exhibition was of interest for a number of things: its unusually heavy attendance of nearly 400,000; the collection of 97 tapestries from a number of places, a collection not really likely to be done more than once or twice a century; and the cooperation it marked between the museums, the Endowment, and foreign governments. It led eventually to the agency's own slice of foreign policy, an agreement with the French government to cooperate in other exhibitions, and understandings with the ministries of other European nations. Aside from the tapestries themselves, which mattered more than anything else, there were new and vitally important aspects of organization. Hoving's statement in the catalog of the exhibition puts the matter in sharp focus:

> These days, with the impression existing that the great international exhibition is passé, the present effort may seem something of an anomaly. Certainly it offers all the characteristics of the supposedly doomed species: splendid loans from all over Europe and the United States, impressive quality throughout, interest for scholars and the general public alike, a distinguished catalogue, focus on a specific moment in the history of art, and, finally, the unstated thought that no one is likely ever to see these particular works together again. Despite appearances, however, this exhibition is less a traditional international loan show than it is a wholly new endeavor. For it is one of the fruits of a partnership worked out a little over a year ago between the Metropolitan Museum and the Réunion des Musées Nationaux of France, including the Louvre.
>
> The partnership came into being as the result of a deep mutual friendship on the part of the professional staffs of both organizations and the recognition that certain museological activities of vital concern to both—great exhibitions, publications related to them, staffing, and even acquisitions of objects—could no longer be handled solo. From this conviction there came a pooling of resources, funds, and powers of persuasion.

The powers of persuasion noted referred to three kinds of initiative: the linkage of museums between nations; the linkage of exhibitions and resources; and the campaign within the Endowment, and between the Endowment and Congress, to make international exhibition a normative part of the agency's work.

Other powers of persuasion were invoked to get Congress to approve yet once more expansion of the total budget. Hat in hand, I came to the committee with the idea that they raise us thirty million dollars. The basic argument was that since we were not being funded up to the limit of our authorization there could be nothing wrong in approaching it. It was a bit tongue in cheek, since authorization limits usually exceed appropriations by almost unimaginable amounts. The passage of an authorization bill signifies that those associated with it have good intentions, and would give the money to the deserving if that were possible. If the federal budget were ever figured in terms of authorization it would amount to two or three times its actual amount.

The new funds were to be measured against the success I had depicted in museums and television; against the mounting flow of applications and, more important, against those applications which our panel judged worth funding; and, nakedly enough, by the organizations, institutions, and other agencies now devotedly part of our constituency. NEH had in fact received more than five thousand applications in the last fiscal year, requesting over one hundred and sixty million dollars. It was this kind of statistic that appealed to OMB, to the White House, and especially to Congress. It would be naive to think that increased funds came from deserved success; from the consequences of cultural investment. One of the prime arguments had to be public interest expressed by application.

The new budget would total ninety-two million dollars, although in deference to the Office of Management and Budget part of that was uncollectible. OMB insisted on a ten-million dollar level of gift and matching funds: one reason being that such funds were listed as part of the federal budget, hence indicated the White House commitment to the program; another, that it could afford to be generous with other people's money, since those gift funds, coming as they did from private sources, cost the Treasury nothing. OMB could take credit simultaneously for economizing and for generosity. Their idea of perfection would of course have been a budget that was entirely gift and matching. There really was no way the Endowment could raise ten million in a single year. The culture industry had begun its current depression. And it was useless to pretend that we were like the Arts Endowment, which had access to two resources not open to us: a field of enterprise which was partly commercial, bringing in substantial amounts of box-office money; and the large sums available from patronage.

The Public Program was scheduled to increase by eleven million dollars, or virtually half its current amount. The increase in was in fact larger than the program when I first found it—and larger than the size of the Endowment first envisioned by its supporters. The lion's share would not go to museums or the film and television divisions: an even stronger political necessity directed it to the State-based program. The official reasons were that State-based grants—actually regrants—would for the first time be available in all fifty states and that the success of the program on the whole justified increased funding. True enough, but the previous authorization hearings had been a warning to spend money in more conventionally political ways.

In order to counterbalance the assumption that NEH was insufficiently social, I emphasized its turnstile statistics. The Humanities Film Forum had done splendidly in bringing Olivier and Guinness to the screen, but was most forcibly persuasive in having thirty million viewers—until that time the fourth-largest audience ever to watch a public television series in this country. The same kind of thing was to be said about *War and Peace.* We had by now logged over a million visitors to the Soviet Impressionist exhibition. And there were by now well over two hundred newspapers running our bicentennial series of lectures, reaching, in all probability, twenty million readers. The Fellowships program was beginning to reach critical mass: we had made approximately one thousand awards in the last year, a figure that meant something even against the universe of those writing and teaching in the humanities.

In short, so far as numbers and the public were concerned, the Endowment seemed to be on its mark. But its accomplishments would have to be judged on the basis of a much wider sampling of programs and individual grants.

CHAPTER VIII

The New Programs

I think it will be helpful to the reader at this point to review a number of representative grants at mid-passage: what the Endowment was doing strategically and tactically as we prepared for yet more growth in 1975. As I've noted in the preceding chapters, the agency had overcome most of its critics, or neutralized their opposition. The question now to be answered was how it conceived of itself: what it *did* while maneuvering between the claims of Congress and its constituency.

Perhaps the best place to start is with the newly-energized Public Division, that part of the Endowment responsible now for State-Based programs, for television, and for assistance to museums. In 1973, the Public Division had been allocated thirty-one percent of agency funds; in 1974 it took thirty-nine percent. Becaus of the mandate of the Joint Authorization Committee of Congress it was now to receive even more: about forty percent of the total NEH budget. According to the wishes of Congress half of that—one-fifth the total budget of the agency—would go to the individual states. The other half of the Public Division's budget, which was comparable to each of the allocations for the divisions of Education, Research and Fellowships, went for television and museums.

The State-Based programs would then absorb $15 million, and would of course increase much more than any other projects under way. So far as I was concerned, this was involuntary; Congress, especially Senator Pell, wanted money distributed to the states. It did not really matter how that money was to be used; what did matter was that large sums would be divided among congressional districts. At this point it may be useful to bring the reader up to date on the mechanisms involved.

All fifty states were by now organized with the NEH State-Based program. Each state was first given a planning grant of from ten to fifteen thousand dollars to cover the costs of nominating committee members and forming an organization. Once these committees became operational they received grants averaging one hundred and sixty-five thousand dollars. The sums for operation were always to increase; eventually removing from professional use about $30 million per year. That was a figure which could in some ways have changed the humanities in academe.

The program was full of contradictions: the congressional purpose being to divide federal funds among the states; Senator Pell's intention being specifically to reward each individual member of the electorate; and my own being to avoid subsidies as far as possible. But the contraption worked. People from libraries, schools, businesses and labor organizations were attracted to the various committees. They did volunteer work, and even raised significant amounts of matching funds on a one-to-one ratio.

These committees tended to conceive of the public interest in terms of public issues. What they really wanted to do was to spend money on what worried them. Alaska, with more land than could be settled, held annual debates with NEH funds on its own capacity to form communities. At the opposite demographic end. Florida used its NEH allotments to debate what it called "The Madding Crowd" of visitors and immigrants to the state. Georgia spent money to discuss its racial history in public forums. Maine talked over its frontier. Nebraska, typical of many other states, was fixated upon its own government. Almost without exception the committees for each state concentrated on issues of growth, race, government and other topics that were narrowly political. There seems to be an exceptionally strong element of self-regard and self-regarding in the American grain. Because of the national habit of looking at every dissatisfaction as if it were a problem, NEH had its work cut out. The idea of the staff was to modify the desire of state committees who used humanities funds to address routine domestic policy. Here is an example from the budget submission of the strange relationship of the humanities and public interests:

> The Indiana Committee for the Humanities functioned in its first year under the general theme: "Government and the Family." It received 57 proposals requesting a total of $275,000, and funded 37 projects with its available funds of $120,000. These grants ranged from $666 to $8,790, involved approximately 200,000 adults and more than 800 professional humanists, and were conducted through such diverse organizations and institutions as community colleges and major 4–year institutions of higher education, an educational television station, two urban public library systems, a county council of churches, several civic and community organizations, and two local humanities committees created for the purpose. Programs included a public lecture and symposium series sponsored by a city government and co-sponsored by eight civic and community organizations which drew a cumulative audience of 15,000 people; two separate series of discussions in senior citizen high-rises with audiences ranging from 25–150 people, focusing on the role of government and place of the elderly in family life, and four public seminars with philosophers, historians, and other humanists discussing "The Crisis of Divorce" with a public audience.

This passage, from the NEH budget submission to the House, indicates the limits of humanistic activity in daily life. In order to reach these audiences or unions or Chambers of Commerce the discourse had to be pitched on a certain level. What the agency was chartered to do was support linguistics, history, philosophy, archeaology, etc., but what the state committees wanted to do was study their own leisure, health care, aging or marital problems. The program engaged the interest of the electorate, but did not, I think, fulfill our charter. When the grantees are considered—The League of Women Voters of Indianapolis, the Family Service Association, Associated

Migrant Opportunity Services—it is only natural to ask whether politics were being humanized or humanities politicized. And, of course, whatever the impulse of Congress, which mandated these activities, one effect was to ennoble the most pragmatic of the social sciences. Not much was being done for poetry. Under the Carter administration the tilt was later exaggerated because NEH by then voluntarily did such things. Anxious not to be suspected of "elitism" the agency itself formulated ways for humanities money to be spent on grantees from the world of social services. The future history of the agency is bound, I think, to be a history of conversions and backsliding on the issue of general public interest, and to what degree that may honestly be translated into humanities grants. At some times both NEH and NEA are bound to be used as viaducts of money to special interests.

As for the other aspects of the Public Division budget, I asked Congress for $6 million for film and television. The use of these things made better sense than rewarding small groups of the general public directly. *So far as I could see, it was preferable to consider the general public as an audience rather than as a collection of potential grantees.* Excellent television shows like *Upstairs, Downstairs* could be produced for relatively little money, and large audiences could easily see them. The price certainly was right, because even though a fifteen-hour television series might cost about $3 million it could reach about 30 million viewers. And that was only for each program—the figure might reach as high as 300 million viewer-hours per series. The outlay per viewer hour came out approximately to one cent.

The Endowment already had such a series in mind. It was to be called The Adams Series and would cover the passage of two centuries in the life of a family embedded in our history. The series was to follow the fortunes of John Adams, John Quincy Adams and Charles Francis Adams from the beginnings of the Republic to the time of Reconstruction after the Civil War. The costs would have been, without an expanded budget, much above us. It cost at least a million for design and staging and more than that for studio facilities. I will be saying more about the reception of this program at an appropriate point.

The Endowment proposed to invest about $5 million in 1975 in museums. This was an increase over the past year of about a hundred percent. Although we had been concentrating on international exhibitions, it would be wrong to imply that these were all the Public Division did. In 1973–1974 grants had gone to many places that would never attract a great deal of public notice: to the Merrimack Valley Textile Museum of North Andover, Massachusetts and to the museums of Wayne State University and the State University College of Oneonta, New York. There are thousands of minor museums and historical associations, and in order for the program to have any kind of institutional depth it had to recognize their existence as well as that of the Met.

The many small museums scattered throughout the country had diverse interests but common problems. They ranged from children's muesums to collections of local archives. But all needed additional funds; had to train their staff and volunteers; needed to make exhibits available to the public; and shared in the national explosion of interest in their *métier*. And most of these, because of the Bicentennial, had assumed a role even larger than that called for by foreseeable demand. The Endowment hoped to do a number of things for these institutions; contribute fellowships for their staff training; and make over funds to train volunteers as well. All of this complemented the great exhibitions at the National Gallery and the Met which were so much more visible.

Higher education was a surprisingly fertile field for our Division of Education Programs not because there was so much done for humanities but because there was so little. Of the thousands of campuses in this country, very few had adequate courses or libraries. For example, of the disciplines listed in the NEH charter only a few could be found outside major universities. Enormous numbers of college-level campuses were—and still are—without modern languages, without classical languages, without really usable libraries. A survey of college catalogs will quickly indicate the relatively small number of disciplines in the humanities which are affordable. It will also indicate that of those disciplines many of the weakest and trendiest courses are representative. It seemed to me that many small colleges were bound to be dissatisfied with this, and with the fact that remedial reading and writing rather than more advanced study were now routine. Out of this situation grew an exceptionally interesting program, designed simply as a form of consultation.

The Education Division sent volunteer scholars and administrators—these included the presidents of both Harvard and Yale—to campuses where they were needed. The volunteers stayed for a week at the place of their assignment and went to countless sessions with local faculty and administrators. They brought with them news of what was happening in the larger world of education, and suggestions for certain improvements. Possibly they brought with them something equally important, a sense of community and mutual recognition. The great thing about this program, it is transparently clear, was that *it did not need money*. That is a fairly important point. The general assumption in the educational world is that money is the *sine qua non* of improvement. But in fact improvement in education is a matter of ideas and assignments. In this case, without any large bureaucratic machinery or expenditure of large amounts of money there was measurable change in the curriculum, in faculty morale, and in awareness of the nature of intellectual work.

There was always residual suspicion in Congress that the Division of Education Programs served only the rich, that its funds went mainly to the Ivy League. Many of the Endowment's fellowships went there, unavoidably, because of the nature of fellowship competition. But the Education Division was designed to serve places outside the circle of elites. There would have been no point in giving Harvard the money to work up a program in history or in literature. But there was a good deal to say for doing that at Abraham Baldwin Agricultural College at Tifton, Georgia; at Albion college in Michigan; and at the Dominican College of San Rafael, California. The fact is, these represented the constituency of the division. And they necessarily represented a problem for the staff: the worse the need for sound programs in the humanities, often the less capacity to install one.

Because of this, the Education division became the most painstaking and client-oriented part of the Endowment. It might take weeks of consultation with the staff to work out a proposal, with applicants coming into Washington and staff going out for extended periods. And it soon became plain that before grants for operation could be made, grants for planning had to be considered. The faculty of small colleges with few resources and no money—either, say, for realistic library collections or for any sabbatical time off for research—needed "released time" for finding out about good courses at major institutions, and modelling their own after them. Planning grants were therefore instituted, if only to make certain that when proposals eventually came in to this division they would be informed, realistic, and bear the evidence of prior thought. It became routine for the division to make out small planning grants, in the vicinity of $10 thousand, and then to expect as a consequence a proposal for large-scale improvement in teaching.

It is worth noting that the Endowment managed to deal, if only in a miniaturized way, with secondary education. It concentrated on the training of teachers and the development of curriculum. For example, a grant to Davidson College in North Carolina enabled it to conduct sizable summer institutes which brought together area-studies specialists from large universities and teachers from local schools. About fifty of the specialists taught some three thousand high school teachers the elements of their subject. A second grant plunged headlong into urban education, financing the study of Latin (successfully, as it turned out) for about a thousand students in the public schools of Washington, D. C.

Many of these grants that I have described brought people from the major leagues to the provinces. One program was designed to do the reverse. The first National Institute for the Humanities, located at Yale, was intended to draw faculty from colleges without research facilities, and return them to their campuses with the kind of training a major university could provide. This kind of institute was purposely located at the best and most prestigious of places. That, I thought, would underline our intentions. Once at an institute, a teacher from a small college would work on ways to bring its ideas to his home institution. He would have his own research to do, and research also on ways of fitting that into the curriculum of his campus.

The Division of Fellowships would appear to have been the simplest to organize because it was the least institutionalized of the agency's components. Fellowships are after all grants to individuals; and it must take a bureaucratic mind *in extremis* to complicate the procedure of application and response. But there were reasons for making things more rather than less complicated. In my view—and I think in the common view—humanities were in a more than economic depression. Teaching was badly done and research seemed not to cope with the institutional problems of learning. I thought that adademics needed some common goals and procedures, and a sense of recognition. A good deal might be accomplished if fellowship, as in the sciences, had common goals; if institutions had more lively connection to each other; if research centers of *all* kinds could be persuaded to take in humanities fellows *en bloc;* if those fellows could work on things demonstrably in their own and the public interest; and if it could be suggested that new fields of enterprise were available at a time when imagination had run low.

With ten million dollars almost all these intentions could be served—as well as the eventualities of application, covering the multitude of good reasons for support known only to their originators. The division would have two main activities: Residential awards, divided among college faculty, summer seminars for teachers, various professions and advanced study; and Independent awards, divided among senior and younger researchers, junior colleges, summer stipends, and some selected fields of inquiry.

Really for the first time in this country enough fellowships would be generated to make a dent in the professional population. There would eventually be over five thousand applications, of which NEH would fund more than a thousand. Because of the multiplier effect which resulted from linking groups of individuals to groups of institutions, like that of the Humanities Institutes in the Division of Education, many teachers and students might be affected. It ought to be recalled that there has never been much money available for humanities research in the United States—in fact, in this respect, whatever the Endowment did would catapult it into the first rank of institutional support.

Our residential fellowships had these ends in view:

1. They were designed to recall the original meaning of "fellowship"—its collegiality and common purpose especially.
2. At the time of their implementation the humanities had from few to no opportunities to link major and lesser institutions.
3. Important common problems for research and teaching had up to this time been left to annual professional meetings. This was intended to transcend occasions and intentions.
4. The structure had some meaning: applicants came from small colleges to a major university, and studied in groups of about twelve under a distinguished scholar whom they would otherwise have known only through libraries. They had a common subject which they worked on in seminars; and enough freedom to respond on their own to the opportunity.
5. The cost was reasonable, about twelve thousand dollars per fellow for the year, with a small amount to cover the overhead for the institution sponsoring the program.

The juxtaposition of host and visiting institutions says something about the spread of education in the United States. Summer seminars were held at Ohio State, Berkeley, Princeton, Charlottesville and other places with big libraries and traditions of research. Their students came from the faculties of Lone Mountain College, Fresno Community College, Middlesex Community College, Adams State, Brandywine College and hundreds of others not on the map of higher learning. Since one of the by-products of the academic depression was diffusion of first-rate people to places which might before this not have invested in them there was a built-in market for our service. Fellowships could now be institutionally useful; an old idea, but with plenty of life to it.

Fellowships should, I thought, be available to intellectuals outside of academe. The reasons are conveniently stated in the budget defense before the House for 1975:

> Leaders in the non-academic professions—journalism, law, medicine, etc.—have an important influence on directions this country takes in all its affairs. Unlike scholars and teachers, whose work involves the advancement and transmission of knowledge, people in the professions are concerned with the *application* of knowledge and have not generally had the time to stand back from their work to examine its philosophical or historical foundations or its wider implications for the community and the nation. Nor have they generally been trained, in the professional schools, to perceive the humanistic dimensions of their work.

The prose is somewhat boilerplate, but the idea is pretty sound. NEH had begun with law and journalism and could now extend humanistic thought and its influence considerably. Lawyers and physicians were natural objects, the latter especially so because of the interest of medical schools in the social problems of scientific advance. It could do no harm to expose journalists to the teaching of humanities at Stanford and Michigan; from what I could determine the emphasis on historical experience led to a more balanced sense of contemporary issues. In a world obsessed by "policy"—which is to say by short-term solutions to long-term problems—the intentions of the agency must have appeared to be exquisitely subliminal. There was, after all, no prescriptive or dogmatic end implied by these courses; and no suggestion of their political application. Fellowships in the professions embodied one of the few big principles of NEH: we could only make people more intelligent; after that they were on their own.

Some of the centers for advanced study in this country have had humanities on their mind, others have for long been devoted to the physical and social sciences alone. By institutionalizing fellowships NEH was able to accomplish certain ends. Research centers changed their minds about the subjects and modes to which they had previously been limited. Scholars in the humanities got the intellectual (and economic) benefits of associating with other fields. And, individuals and institutions could be linked in new ways, with NEH at their center. The program brought humanities to places dominated by other fields, like the Center for Advanced Study in the Behavioral Sciences at Stanford. It created a place for them at the Woodrow Wilson International Center in Washington, D. C. And it suggested both new and conventional associations at The American Academy in Rome, the Metropolitan Museum, and the Newberry Library. Not the least of the benefits to be expected were those to the agency itself, for it now acted as a clearning-house for projects and ideas and could function as more than a mechanism of government.

Among the many fascinations of the Division of Research were its grants to projects literally engaged in the discovery of knowledge. In archaeology, it participated in the reconstruction of the Roman port of Ostia, the discovery of ancient Sybaris, the reconstruction of the oldest known ship, revealed by digs on Cypress, the classification and interpretation of the cave paintings of Lascaux and Altamira. The editing of manuscripts is less exciting, except when, at the end of years of accumulation and study a subject like Jefferson appears. In its own way editing is the discovery of knowledge. It now involves fairly massive undertakings: many scholars joined in an enterprise that takes many years. Some of the best work at our universities has been of this kind, and has resulted in editions of Johnson, Boswell, Milton and More. The Endowment was especially interested in American editions like the *Papers of*

George Washington which fulfilled our Bicentennial vows; as well as the papers of Webster, Robert Morris and other Founders; and of Booker T. Washington, Jane Addams, John Dewey and dozens of other founders of modern culture.

We don't often think of discovery as one of the things native to humanities—that being left pretty much to the realms of physical science. But the materials for reinterpretation of the past are a resource of discovery—if they could but be assembled. The historical archives of our states and cities have been stupendously neglected. Many irreplaceable records dealing with land transactions, immigration, law; many of the statistics we think vital; and nearly all the original forms of our historical knowledge of the past are in documentary form; and in that form they have been mutilated, ignored, stored away and forgotten, and subjected to every conceivable offense of time. The State and Local History Program of the Division of Research funded preservation of these papers, as well as all the various ways of using and interpreting them. In Houston, Texas the Division funded a center for local history that recovered papers scattered among businesses, civic groups and the back files of many local agencies. They were as lost to the world in these files, or moldering in boxes in church basements, as if they had never been known. Another project, in Ohio, is described in the tenth annual report of the agency to the President:

> A coalition of the Ohio Historical Society, the Ohio AFL-CIO, the Ohio State University, and the Ohio Network of American History Research Centers is making the first serious attempt to document the long neglected contribution of labor to the state of Ohio. With initial NEH support, a team of historians and archivists is locating, depositing in repositories around the state, and cataloguing the records of labor unions, labor councils, and all district and city councils as well as those personal papers, printed materials, and audiovisuals involving workers. Extensive interviews are being conducted to supplement the record with taped oral histories.

One other project deserves some notice, the grant to the Maryland Hall of Records Commission for the extraordinary history it had mounted, from 1635 to 1789, of the make-up, income, economic motives, education, social background and values of the state legislature. This was Namier-history of the most practical kind and would almost certainly do more for the Bicentennial than any amount of celebration.

Defense of the budget was in one particular case made a good deal easier by the public reception it enjoyed. *TIME* ran a page of Courses By Newspaper, which were by now running amok in the national press. These courses had begun in a handful of local newspapers and were now being carried by nearly three hundred. The general public benefitted from them as a mass audience, which was, I thought, the best strategy for grants in the largest public interest. This grant, like some others to museums, was widely noted. By now the Courses By Newspaper had a standard format. A course would consist of twenty "lectures" or columns printed every Thursday in newspapers across the country. Their combined circulation was nearly 20 million. The lectures were done by CBN "faculty" like Oscar Handlin of Harvard, Henry C. Wallich of Yale, and Philip Morison of M.I.T. The courses covered history, psychology, sociology, political science—in short, most of the curriculum of a decent university. The views advanced were not those of the management, which in the strict sense had no views at all. The real interest of the project was that it gave the public a chance, at virtually no cost, to read high wuality material ordinarily reserved for the great universities. And, of course, it made a slight dent in newspapers, occasionally replacing an astrology column or advice to the lovelorn with thoughts on other things.

The budget for 1975 was successful in Congress, and these and other grants had another year's lease of life. Julia Hansen was joined in retirement by Alan Bible, to whom belong the last words in this chapter:

> Mr. Berman: I would like to end, Senator, with a few words, that I think are especially worthwile. That is, sums

appropriated by the Senate to the growth of our agency have depended upon the good judgment of Senator Alan Bible. We are grateful for that and we hope that, even in retirement, he will be at least moderately proud of his work for the endowments.

Senator Bible: Well, that is a good statement to make when you are trying to get a 60 percent increase. I appreciate your sentiment. We just labor and do the best we can.

CHAPTER IX

Grants Good and Bad

I have so far discussed many of the grants made by NEH as it developed and, unavoidably, emphasized their success. But of course not all grants were successful. It is sometimes harder to give money away usefully than it is go get it. In this chapter I will take up several kinds of institutional failure.

It's important to realize that success and failure can be relative: that a grant which has every earmark of intellectual quality and public effectiveness may be a political disaster. We might begin by looking at a grant which was popular, admired by the press, appreciated by its recipients. The project began with the desire of Brooklyn College and the Brooklyn Academy of Music to invite the Royal Shakespeare Company to New York for a series of performances. It seemed to the Endowment that the proposal ought to be expanded. The Royal Shakespeare need not confine its activities to performance, and need not stay only in New York. In fact, under the original conditions of application, the proposal would have had to be referred to the Arts Endowment.

A number of changes were suggested: chief among them that when the Royal Shakespeare visited Brooklyn College or any other campus it should become involved in the teaching of drama. Rather than visit a campus it might become part of one. Rather than perform exclusively for paying audiences it might do so for large numbers of students without the price of admission. The eventual plan was for the Royal Shakespeare to move from East to Midwest, and take up residence briefly on campuses in Nebraska and Colorado.

One might think that all this was ideal: we had two regional universities, the University of Denver and the University of Nebraska at Omaha as beneficiaries and stout supporters. The media were much impressed by the idea of combining the performance and the teaching of drama by members of the cast. But even before the grant began its operation I was notified by Senator Pell's office that it would not do. Both labor and management in the theatre business had complained. Not about the purpose or the effect of the grant, but because the Royal Shakespeare was in competition with American box-office.

Actor's Equity was the main adversary. It stated to the press that the Humanities Endowment was putting American artists out of work; that federal money was leaving our borders; and that I was a contributing factor to the ruin of the American theater. So much for cultural exchange. It did not do any good to point to the facts, which were that the agency was paying for the teaching, and not for the performance—or that our grantees were the Universities of Denver and Nebraska, which seemed to have the right to apply for whatever they chose.

The project itself proceeded beautifully. A quarter of a million dollars were raised among the three locations, New York, Denver and Omaha, because the grant was attractive for gift-and-matching funds. The Royal Shakespeare made evidently memorable appearances, and did a hard-working job in residency. Much of this was retold to me a year later, when I happened to visit Omaha, and the numbers of sources seemed to indicate no less than the truth.

From Clive Barnes in the *Times* to the *Omaha World-Herald* the reception was warm. As for me, the reception was even warmer. Thomas Fischandler of the Washington Arena Stage complained bitterly to those he know in Congress and effectively set them on me. He called a press conference in which NEH was lambasted *in absentia*. The next day, on the theory that he had made an impression, he called me to ask for a grant.

Another representative of the theatre industry, Alexander Cohen, came to the Endowment from New York to continue the campaign. In order to atone, the Humanities Endowment was asked to subsidize tickets for *other* performances, to pay for American productions exported to Europe, and to do a variety of other things directly benefitting the industry. In short, NEH was to learn the same lesson that NEA had, which was that benefits could be paid only to constituents. And of course that is the reason why NEA has for so long been diplomatically silent on the matter of cultural exchange: it has been forcibly prevented from that by a combination of theatre and congressional power.

The matter was vigorously pressed by Actor's Equity. As the unions saw this issue, they could not afford to allow universities or foundations to engage in box-office cultural exchange. And the unions won. Representative Giaimo, who stood for Stratford, Connecticut, insisted that I write a letter of apology to the union. And I was invited to his office for what turned out to be a comedy of errors. Upon arrival I was asked why NEH did nothing for national values, why ditto for the national crisis, and why our money should leave these shores. I was asked also why the agency had no program for inflation and unemployment. It was clear that all of this was drama itself. Possibly the high point of the discussion was reached when I was accused of putting American actors out of work by bringing over Olivier's *Henry V* for another project, the Humanities Film Forum. I was able to reply, happily, that the film had been made before the questioner—a routinely obnoxious and parasitical congressional aide—had been born. But, we genuflected before the powers. It is therefore possible for a good grant to be a bad grant.

There is of course the bad grant which never has a possibility of being good. Of that, let me give some examples. There is first the responsibility of the Endowment itself, which worried about how to use all of its new money. The Public Division began something called Program Development Centers in order to develop ideas and projects which might later be funded. In other words, not only was the Endowment coming up with intentions best left to its applicants—it was also creating its own grantees. The sole duty of these "Centers" was to originate ways of spending money. In fact, the scripts and films and workshops espoused by these groups did manage to spend as much money as had been anticipated—but rarely produced a *product* of any value. One of the great institutional ways of wasting money is to do a film about practically anything.

The Public Division had managed in its unconscious way to create miniatures of government. It had produced bureaucracies which worked hard and conscientiously to no purpose. At rather substantial expense they attracted ideas meant only to absorb funds.

A second example reflects the spirit of the age, at least in education. A group of faculty from Syracuse University came up with an idea which they were sure would invalidate traditional practices of teaching. A program of courses in English Literature would be funded which would be broken down to eight levels of achievement. Instead of all students taking the same course and being graded on the same basis, they would take eight versions, and be graded in eight different ways—or, better put, by eight different standards. As I puzzled over the vocabulary of this proposal, with its emphasis on "downward revision" and "flexibility" and credit for "unstructured" study like going to the movies a certain amount of the implication sunk in: instead of a single scale of achievement there always, in this program, would be a level beneath which it was impossible to sink. The idea was completely ingenious: inventing a course with different standards of grading so that no minority could ever be offended, and no student of whatever race or sex failed. This was the type of grant that really did represent the world-spirit, and really would have pleased many of the Endowment's constituents. It had been funded, unknown to me, and we lived with it.

It was rare for either the Administration or the Congress to flog grants for favorites, but it did happen. And these grants were invariably bad. That is to say, they had no connection with our charter; only with the force that could be exerted on our budget. The most catastrophic of these began to unwind when a lobbyist well recommended by Members of the House appeared at my office with a project for a film to be made on the lives of Congressmen in office. The pretences were many and ingenious, among them that this film would show government in action and humanize the study of civics. It was of course a transparent dodge, intended to win the support of incumbents who would quickly see in what ways it immortalized them. The script, done from interviews with prominent Members of the House, was a jumble of anecdotes and self-flattery.

Tip O'Neill, the Majority Leader, became interested in the benefits of the project and invited me to talk it over in his office. It is not usual for heads of agencies of this derisory size to be invited to the office of the Majority Leader. After a brief wait, which I spent talking to his various assistants, he appeared, having come down from the floor disgusted with the world and needing to be put in humor. His first sentence turned everyone pale, including his assistants: it was about the 93rd Congress, and what a smashing job it had done unhorsing Richard Nixon; establishing once more the power of the Legislative Branch which now was to see itself doing all this on film. Dead silence is hardly the phrase for the situation: a Republican administration, now under Gerald Ford, being invited to donate millions to a subject which would re-ignite every controversy of the past two years. I caught the Majority Leader before he could launch into sentence two, and did a tremendous *ad lib* number on the history of Congress and how the film should reach into the past of the Founding Fathers and away from the truly diabolical politics of the present moment. I orated for five minutes, and produced a grateful glaze in every eye. The staff of the Endowment and the Majority Leader's assistants looked like the Seven Sleepers. But when they awoke all agreed that, if present politics could be got out of the way, we could deliver a nice little film on our national history of legislation. We could move it back a hundred years, and take the sting out of its tail.

But it turned out badly after all. The Majority Leader had an aide who wanted to produce this mess. All I could hope for was that it would be a film which, like all its kind, would be stored safely away after having bored its audience, pleased its subject, and enriched its makers. No such luck: the project was designed to become a television series, royally expensive; a gleam in its producer's eye and a beam in everyone else's. It was left to the Carter Administration to deal with this after my resignation. They stood and delivered.

Sometimes, however, a good deal could be salvaged from our collisions with the magnates of the Congress. One day, in the midst of House Appropriations hearings in 1976, the proceedings were interrupted by a telephone call from George Mahon, the estimable and very senior chairman of the full House Committee. He was audibly upset about an NEH bicentennial grant to the city of San Antonio. He had been informed—and this turned out to be true enough—that Endowment money given to the local Bicentennial Committee had been regranted to the San Antonio Gay Alliance. It made quite a stir in Texas. Texas has its own worldview, and no one aspiring to an education in politics should miss acquaintance with it. I told Mahon, who asked me to his office, that review of the proposal had been done by local citizens in his own state to whom we had given bloc control of Bicentennial funds. He wanted to know why NEH had not reviewed the grant, and I said it was inconsistent with local responsibility: and, that we trusted municipal groups to do right by us. We couldn't make much of the matter—he had to do something for his constituents and I had nothing to say that would remotely satisfy them, not even the truth. In a very diplomatic way, however, Mahon solved the issue. He showed up at our hearings, for the first time in living memory. It was of course absurd, because the total annual budgets of NEH and its sister agency amounted to a tiny fraction of one percent of the Federal Budget—enough, perhaps, for part of one aircraft carrier. But there he was, in this tiny room with a group of bureaucrats and reformed professors, on the record for his constituents in Lubbock and his supporters in San Antonio. And he gravely informed us that for making this silly grant we would be docked one million dollars. Texas was highly satisfied, and so was the agency. The cut came out of gift-and-matching funds, leaving them still several millions beyond the point to which they would eventually be cut at our own request. As I've noted earlier, the agency was always saddled with an impossibly high target of such funds by the Office of Management and Budget. In the depressed educational economy it was always difficult and sometimes impossible for us to raise gift-and-matching money, and we were always grateful for cuts in the requirement. It was good to know that Mr. Mahon could perform two such different services at the same time.

By its own fault, the Endowment blundered into a genuinely bad grant, and was burned badly in the media for it. At the same time as the intervention by Mr. Mahon, and for the reason that yet another Bicentennial grant had miscarried, the *New York Times* attacked the agency's policies. I was informed by William Safire—a friend of mine—that he would pillory us for having wasted an enormous amount of money upon an idiocy. The Endowment had granted rather a lot of money, almost a quarter of a million dollars, to the American Library Association so that it could draw up a book list for general observance of the nation's two-hundredth birthday. The amount of money was ridiculous—and so was the booklist. And I was uniquely responsible, for I knew that beforehand, told the members of the staff that, and then let them argue me down. I told them that I could draw up the list, or an equivalent, in fifteen minutes for no money at all, and they told me that such a list needed the imprimatur of an official library association—and besides, that it would do libraries a world of good. I paid for my toleration. Of course the librarians went wild with the chance to make themselves "relevant." They came up with a reading list as silly as Safire said it was: a concoction of titles on pop psychology, revisionist history and radical chic. After reading it, one would know that the Founding Fathers loved war, slavery and money; and that the United States was responsible for everything from the Cold War to migraine headache. The librarians had gotten their information from flacks and publishers. They justified their choices by pointing out that these books were the latest trend. As a reading list it was merely laughable; as an exercise in scholarship, deplorable: and as a government initiative it was stupid beyond words.

Safire and then another friend of mine, Pat Buchanan, nailed the agency to the cross in their columns. *TV Guide* shed some crocodile tears on the subject. *The Wall Street Journal*, always a strong supporter of mine, sliced us up nicely on its editorial page. The whole experience was very salutory and encouraged me to think about putting all of the agency's money into an interest-bearing account in Switzerland for the remainder of my term.

Finally an intellectually interesting case of failure. This affected the most popular programs that NEH offered, those which supported museum exhibitions. The Endowment had helped underwrite the costs of nearly every blockbuster exhibition from 1972 to 1976: from the Soviet to the Chinese to the Tutankhamun shows. It had produced a wave of genuine gratitude in the public, and an immense amount of favorable footage in the media. But these shows also produced a highly unfavorable response in the critics. Lead by Hilton Kramer, critics now began to argue that large exhibitions should not be held. They attracted too many people; they distracted the museums from their own proper duties; they incurred expenses that were evitable; they substituted fanfare for meditation; they blocked off museums from serious study; and they involved far too much historical apparatus. In short, the critics had two essential views: that certain things were wrong with the way great exhibitions were produced, and that they would very much like to shut out the general public.

It took me a while to get used to this particular punishment, for I had been convinced—and remained so—that great exhibitions mattered. It was good for a huge public audience to be generated, and for rare works of art to circulate. But since the beginning of the great sequence of exhibitions there has been a kind of dialogue of porcupines on the subject. The critics have had some good points: among them that certain works of art should not travel. But their attack seems to be mounted upon a reprehensible strategy, that of keeping crowds out of museums.

Future scholars will want to make case studies not only of the successes of the Humanities Endowment but of such failures as I have indicated here. My own sense of the matter is that the potentiality for failure is inherent. The two Endowments will always be subject to political pressure, which must routinely be fought off. They will always blunder—the Arts Endowment will always make a grant for some absurd poem that everyone else hates, and the Humanities Endowment will always make some constituency unhappy by satisfying another.

CHAPTER X

The Politics of Culture

From the beginning of its legislated existence the National Endowment for the Humanities found itself in conflict with the Administration, Congress, and with its own constituency. Our grantees were grateful for our services, but most of them would have preferred a steady flow of federal subsidy. They did not like to make repeated applications, and it was their dream to become line-items on the Federal Budget: mandated recipients of funds given by entitlement. The Administration was the least of our difficulties, except that it routinely tried, and increasingly succeeded, in making appointments to the National Council on the Humanities dependent purely upon political affiliation. Congress was the greatest of our difficulties, not because it exhibited many direct improprieties or tried to influence the giving of grants to specific individuals or institutions but because it tried consciously and continuously to divert the budget of the agency away from professional and towards public benefits.

If I may for the moment briefly review the congressional situation: in the Senate, Claiborne Pell, who controlled the legislation governing the agency, had tried since its inception to convert the humanities into a form of cultural welfare. He wanted five percent of the funds given to individual citizens without college training. Such funds would be divided among "grocers" and "lumberjacks" (the terms were his own, often alluded to in hearings, statements to the press, on the floor of the Senate) in order to provide them with after-hours enjoyment of the great books. Each grocer and each lumberjack would receive five hundred dollars to do so. In addition, Senator Pell wanted another twenty percent of the agency's funds to go directly to the states each year. It did not especially matter what these funds produced; what mattered only was the audience they reached. They were to be assigned to citizen's committees on the humanities in each of the fifty states.

The power of the sub-committee Chairman was such that

the agency had to comply. And, until 1976, there was a workable compromise. NEH funded a group of such citizen's committees, having first made sure that they were composed of teachers, librarians, curators, and other professionals. These groups were encouraged to apply for funds annually to the mother agency, and to spend such funds on education. By 1976 such groups were operational in all fifty states and, while I did not think of them as ideal solutions to the problem I did believe that they were moderately successful. On the negative side, the work they did was sometimes indistinguishable from general social discourse. They loved to sponsor public debates on over-population, divorce, alcoholism and other anxieties. They spent much money on their own little bureaucracies. They funded projects that did not do much for the advancement of the humanities. On the positive side, they were all volunteer, and so took no salaries. They raised impressive amounts of local gift-and-matching money. They sent money to community colleges, libraries and civic associations. They became enthusiasts, and lobbied for the agency whenever a congressional district needed to express approval of our operations.

Senator Pell insisted on more direct political benefits. He wrote into the law the requirement that NEH, like NEA, had to give away twenty percent of its budget each year to citizen's committees in each state. He insisted that the governor of each state appoint the members of those committees. In short, he wished to make them political entities which would be adversaries of the Endowment, and he succeeded in accomplishing that.

It might be noted that there was nothing in the charter which suggested all this. At no time during the current change in legislation was it implied that, by doing this, teaching might be improved, research sustained, or libraries, universities and museums benefitted. The policy had no object of making education in the humanities better or even more available. It was simply a means to insure a flow of cash from Washington to the states.

The usual way for laws to take shape is for consultation to

occur between Congress, lobbyists, and the Executive agencies involved. But only the first two took part in deliberations this time. Before I knew anything about the intentions of Senator Pell he had put draft language into our new authorization bill. It stipulated that the entire State-Based program be replaced by state humanities "councils," which is to say by state bureaucracies. These did not exist, and would have to be called into existence. I found that NEH had been lied to by the Senator and his staff. After assurances that all was going well with our bill I found that there would be hearings with hostile witnesses who would incorporate themselves into "councils" as soon as the law was passed. There is a difference between giving everyone his day in court and allowing the fox into the chicken coop.

Information had been withheld, the provisions of the new law had been covered up, and the agency was to be stripped of a large part of its funds. I made the tactical error of letting Pell and his staff know that I knew this. Although lies are common enough in Congress this one was embarrassing. It had been called, and the Senator's stock in trade was morality. He had several choices, one of them being to tell the truth. Another, as is the way with Congress, was to patch things over without bothering much about right or wrong. He decided instead to demand that the White House not re-appoint me to a second term as Chairman.

I did not at first take him seriously, underestimating his power and malice, the weakness of the new Ford administration, and the privileges allowed by the Senate to its members. The grounds of the Senator's complaint to the White House Personnel Office were that I did not manage well, was power-mad, and ran a poor State-Based Program. Since he had made it his business annually to praise me in the pages of the *Congressional Record* for both management and character it made an odd lot of accusations.

In an effort to extract my nomination for a second term from the White House I reminded the President's staff that Pell had no claim on their affections. They told me that neither did I. They might actually stand to gain by placating a prominent Democrat, and vacating an office which patronage might fill once more.

It seemed to me that planning to lose a conflict was a poor way to enter it. If the White House did give in gracelessly then members of the National Council on the Humanities would resign, the staff of the agency would become demoralized, and every politico in Washington would know that the Endowment could be shaken down. And in fact, a few days after I conveyed that, Sidney Hook, a prominent member of the Council said that he would indeed resign if I had to leave.

My congressional aide got to Pell's office meanwhile, and found one of the reasons for his malaise. Pell had been so embarrassed by the mail and calls coming in to his office, most of which he had solicited in favor of his new amendment, that only my blood could wash away the offense. It seems that his friends and consultants, of whom there were many, agreed with me about the State-Based Program, and disagreed with him about the management of NEH.

The malignancy took a year or so to develop. Early in October of 1976 the Senator caught up with Robert Goldwin, who was to the Ford White House in some respects what Leonard Garment had been to the Nixon Administration, and informed him that I was to be charged with certain things. First, that the agency had failed an audit by the General Accounting Office. Pell tended to blunder in these things, and unhappily found the next day that NEH had in fact passed the audit; it being recommended by the GAO that the Chairman be given even more authority than the law presently allowed. After this the Senator accused me of having lost the confidence of the Council and demanded a poll on my re-appointment. Twenty out of twenty-one insisted that I be re-appointed. He was mortified, and looked for other charges.

Frank Vandiver, Vice-Chairman of the Council, met with Robert Goldwin early on the 4th of November 1975 and then spent the afternoon with Senator Pell. The morning interview went well, it having been established that the White House, which had no real stake in my appointment, could not find any reasons *not* to go ahead with it. But the meeting with Senator

Pell was somewhat different. Although Frank Vandiver had been able to supply a rebuttal for every accusation, the Senator kept to his assertions: that my relationships with the Council were poor, that the Endowment was badly run, and the State-Based Program ineffective. He found no difficulty in contradictions: that the Council had recently requested my re-appointment, and that the State-Based Program had won the support of his own consultants. Frank found the Senator's reaction in excess of the facts, and we both supposed that it had not much relation to them. The next day my name went up to the Personnel Office for a new term on the job.

I met with Jack Javits in his office the same day. He, too, disliked the State-Based Program but we quickly found a compromise: the committees would remain voluntary but the members would be annually re-appointed, some of them by the Governor of each state. Javits promised to back my appointment and to persuade Pell to it. I left feeling not too badly about things. But, a day or so later three of the ablest Council members went to see Pell and he put them through the wringer, now threatening to sever the two Endowments, cut our budget and punish the agency in other ways for my misdeeds.

I then went up to see Pell, answered his charges and listened while he complained that his own committee disagreed with him about my appointment. I soothed him, and said that I'd much rather win with his cooperation than over his dead body; all very appropriate for the face-saving involved. I went over everything, but succeeded only in settling the issues. He did not want the issues settled.

There was a good talk with John Brademas a few days later. Al Quie and John Brademas were to my mind never to be praised enough; as the situation developed it was only the House that kept our bill from being the kind of punishment that Pell had in mind.

Next day, the 13th of November, I went up before the Senate for the authorization hearing. Pell began with a statement of his beliefs, without referring to the evidence that had nullified them. There was the now-predictable passage on grocers and shoemakers; and some alarming disenchantment with academics and intellectuals. He complained continuously at the waste of money on an educated elite. I managed to avoid questions intended to entrap me by ignoring them in the hope that they would sink out of sight in the closed committee hearings. My strategy was to take away the initiative whenever possible. When the Senator made personal remarks I let them go; when he carped at the agency I combined respect and contradiction. When he stumbled about I changed the subject. Nancy Hanks and John Brademas bucked me up on the performance.

Shortly after this I met Barry Goldwater who said that he was having a rough time convincing Pell. He told me that Bill Baroody, President of the American Enterprise Institute and a great stalwart, had been on the phone a half-hour with him over this. Goldwater was not optimistic. Don Rumsfeld, Secretary of Defense, was brought in as a friend of the court by Len Garment and Bill Buckley. Bob Goldwin called, somewhat embarrassed by having to ask my political registration. The White House was under the impression that I was not a Republican, which may have accounted for some of the difficulties. Bob was as ever very helpful, but I could not quite believe the implications. I hoped they had Brezhnev on file under the Soviet Union.

Another audit for NEH: Pell was fighting now with every weapon at his command. He insisted that the nomination be delayed—for months—while the audit was under way. I refused, and told the White House we had to go ahead with it or have it die of inertia. But Goldwin got the same story from the head of the White House Personnel Office. The good news was that Pell had now withdrawn his charges. The audit, delay and Senatorial privilege were all he had left; they were probably enough.

Until this time Livingston Biddle, Pell's assistant, had tried to mediate; now, recognizing that his principal was immoveable, and that he had only two choices, he decided to humor the patient. Pell and Biddle claimed to the White House and to the media that NEH was not as successful as the Endowment for the Arts, at least as measured by coverage and approval of the media. It was true enough; but of course the same could have been said of the National Science Foundation. I couldn't do much with Pell and Biddle, but did get to see Jack Javits and explain the difference between visibility and presence. The first was the effect of a performance on the media. The second was the effect of thought in society. Thought is not really an event, and what the humanities do is not visible to the naked eye. Javits saw the distinction, and agreed that NEH should not be held accountable for having a less enthusiastic press than the Arts. We talked about the full partnership of the two agencies, and especially about parity in their budgets. Javits was pleasantly surprised to see how much we did for New York, probably a deciding factor for him.

There was more from Bob Goldwin on the tenth of the month: the nomination was pretty well stuck in the White House Personnel Office. Bill Baroody went to work on it once more. It became clear that the White House would not help out, even to the extent of getting Pell's committee on my side.

Both conservatives and liberals had recently attacked the agency's policies, especially those which tended to popularize culture. There was no reason for them not to do so. But common sense urged an equilibrium between public and professional benefits. Neither should dominate: not promoting research too narrow for public funding, nor the political distribution of money to every one who wanted it. But Pell now issued a committee report affecting the agency itself, urging that the culture of "tens of millions of Americans" become our major aim. This might be either no culture at all, or several cultures too many. If the idea was to bring humanities to as many people as possible that was well enough. But if it meant giving money to voters without asking too many questions about how it would be used that was something else.

I thought the meaning was clear. Pell was in a lather of anti-intellectualism, willing to confuse professionalism with elitism, and ultimately looking for a stick to beat a dog. Whatever we were not doing was his ground for complaint.

In early January 1976 Goldwin told me that Pell had spoken

to the Congressional Liaison Office of the White House and restated his opposition to my appointment. I was told by a friend in the White House bureaucracy that I would be kept in limbo until after the presidential election. My name would not after all be sent up to the Senate for confirmation. It was enormously depressing.

But there was a radical alteration on the seventh: the day beginning with Senator Buckley phoning me at home to ask how he could help out. I talked to him several times, and he told the White House what he expected of them. By the close of business that day the cork had popped out of the bottle. He must have been marvelously firm: I was left for dead on Monday, gave up on Tuesday, and found by Wednesday that I was scheduled for nomination within two weeks. I knew that there would be a formidable coalition of conservatives and liberals on the case; and I suspected a tremendous send-off from the media.

The disproportion between power and logic was sometimes pretty funny. Pell was free to say anything he wanted, but could make almost nothing stick. The week that he began his campaign on the invisibility of the agency both *Time* and *Newsweek* devoted more space to the *Adams Family Chronicle* than to the presidency. It was a mad success in Washington, drawing the sympathy of almost everyone in public life; and appreciation from those who followed the development of public television. The object now was to intensify public appreciation for NEH, and there were good responses from columnists like John Roche, Nick Thimmesch, Max Frankel and Anne Crutcher, all of whom planned to cover the case. *The New York Times* was sympathetic, but not to the point of running an editorial against a senator who had for so long embodied its views. *The Washington Post* simply maintained silence; the issue being invisible to them for the whole course of things. I thought their indignation over fair practices in government mightily selective. The issue was not after all whether they agreed with me, but only whether a hearing could be infinitely postponed, so that neither side could be stated in an accountable way.

At the same time, the third week in January 1976, the second GAO audit came to a close. I met with the five auditors and my Deputy, Robert Kingston, and was a witness to one of the great performances of the bureaucracy fighting back. Kingston had mastered the entire procedure, and knew more about the report than those who had made it. He uncovered every flaw mercilessly, and got the auditors to admit their humiliation over the covert intention of the investigation and the way it had been carried out. They agreed to conclude that there was nothing unfavorable to me or NEH, and one more of the obstacles had disappeared. For intelligence and rarely-appropriate moral indignation Kingston couldn't be topped; a nice moment in our finale.

Irving Kristol and many others converged on the AFL-CIO to get the endorsement of Lane Kirkland and George Meany. There was an hilarious afterthought: the unions wrote Pell that since our State-Based Program did so much for labor organizations, and had so many contacts with their members, it should be left exactly as it was. Arthur Hertzberg, former President of the American Jewish Congress, saw one of the key men in the mess, Harrison Williams, chairman of Pell's full committee. Williams would ultimately decide whether to judge the case on its merits or by the rules of senatorial courtesy.

The Adams show continued to attract the media, *Times, Post* and *Star* giving it enormous praise for the rest of the month. A long piece on the politics of the appointment came out in the *Star,* in which I was accused of reluctance to support nonsense, of being unwilling to politicize the Endowment or to chase publicity; not impeachable offenses. The article also mentioned that NEH had passed its audit with flying colors. I was clearly ahead in every respect except that of dealing with the powers and privileges of the Senate.

I had the first of many long talks with Arthur Krim, who supported me from his vantage point in Democratic politics. The American Jewish Committee weighed in, sending its chief lobbyist, Hy Bookbinder, to the Hill to argue the case. Although the usual thing in Washington is for a man to twist slowly in the wind, this matter became an honorable exception.

Wherever I looked, people spoke up to disregard the custom of the place.

There were good talks with John Brademas, who undertook to carry things to Pell; with a former Council member, Bob Ward of Stanford, who knew that it would be important to see Alan Cranston; and even with people from the Arts Endowment. And there was a not especially good talk with Pell on the 29th of January, which really did bring some things out in the open.

I spent about a half-hour with him, going over the *Adams Family Chronicle*, and drawing the admission that this grant had served those "tens of millions of Americans" he had in mind. He added that he liked me personally, but was going to block my appointment. He would do that by tabling the nomination in his sub-committee and preventing a vote on it, or passage to the Senate floor. More or less at his wit's end to find a reason for this, he said that his standard of reappointment was now "exceptionally outstanding" performance—and whereas I had only been outstanding, I could not hope for another term. I was tempted to ask him for his opinions on service in the Senate. At any rate, it seemed pretty clear that he was determined to find or invent some criterion that I could not exceed. He left briefly for a roll-call, and Livingston Biddle then tried to blackmail me into submission.

Biddle suggested that I would be vulnerable to public charges about my administration of the agency, that a confrontation with so virtuous a Senator would ruin my character, and that it would be safest for me to depart and head some fortunate university. I suggested that if it came to being defeated in committee the Senator might change his mind. Biddle said that the GAO report would give Pell whatever he needed to damage me—and with some incredulity I asked if he knew what was in it. He did not. When I told him that the auditors had agreed not to criticize me, and suggested only a few cosmetic improvements in office procedures, he was visibly shocked. As I left the office my congressional liaison aide was somewhat upset, and told me that the Senator had offered him a job in his own office if he would get off the case.

Andrew Biemiller, sent over by the AFL-CIO to help me, was offered a compromise by Pell: I could stay on the job until the election. Since that was no compromise at all I asked the unions to press somewhat harder for a hearing. Senator Cranston gave a flat assurance to Caroline Ahmanson, our Council member from Los Angeles, that he would support me; had he kept his word I might now be making grants instead of writing about them. I was worried about Javits because he had close personal and political ties with Pell. But his constituents were hot and heavy after him to support me.

I was invited over to the Rayburn Building to talk to Frank Thompson, one of the founders of NEH legislation. I hadn't realized that his interest began as early as 1955, a decade before anything actually happened. Thompson went over Pell's opposition to my appointment, and we talked about the reasons first raised to oppose me and their abandonment. Thompson said, much to his credit, that he and John Brademas would actively campaign for me. It was a fine gesture—much more than a gesture—from a man not actively involved on any of the Endowment's committees, and on the other side of the political fence. He gave me good advice if I should ever get out of this, to spend more time on the Hill mending that fence.

I had another long session with the GAO auditors, who proved to be decent men. They had corrected everything called to their attention by Bob Kingston, and wanted me to know that the report in its final form had nothing damaging to me. They thought, however, that it might be used out of context. They regretted that; so did I.

I visited John Brademas on the 6th of February; he had seen Pell but been rebuffed. We both foresaw a conflict now, to be won by me with as little show of force as possible. A good strategy for keeping the support of the Senate while fighting the privilege of a Senator; but it didn't work in Korea or Viet Nam. Then to Jack Javits; and at that point I took some relief in what he could say. He undertook to handle my confirmation in committee, even though he too had been rebuffed by Pell. He felt sure of Harrison Williams, the great unknown. Javits advised me not to let up on contact with committee members, and to have the nomination delivered to the Senate as soon as possible. He agreed that Pell's opposition was irrational, but felt that it had to be handled tenderly. Javits was very intelligent, with an eye for my media support and the cowardice of the White House.

The media response that had developed and was to come still strikes me as remarkable. Senator Pell began by literally charging that the Endowment, when judged by its press clippings, failed the test of publicity. He dropped this charge with some anguish as the issue generated skyrockets and barrages of coverage, almost all in favor of his opposition. He later replaced this charge with the complaint that the press had become captive to the agency.

Some of the press coverage came from newspapers and journals unknown to me and was simply based on the issues. Some came from writers who were both friends and associates: John Roche had been a Council member before my term and understood the issues. Anne Crutcher of *The Washington Star* had been a panelist, and wrote with superb intelligence about the agency's purpose and situation. Jeffrey Hart was appointed to the Council by President Nixon, and was deeply motivated by shared ideas and very close friendship. Their coverage was in itself a political spectrum: John Roche was on Lyndon Johnson's White House staff and a former President of ADA; Jeffrey Hart is an editor of *National Review*. There was in addition a third force, a kind of one-man gang: Roger Rosenblatt, who had left the Education Division of NEH to become Literary Editor of the *New Republic*. Because of him the *New Republic* joined *National Review*, at least on this issue, and quite frankly drove Senator Pell crazy with its anger and wit.

The conflict with Pell awakened all kinds of sleeping dogs. The agency was now perceived to be weak, and ready for plundering. One Congressman took me to task because NEH grants were being given only to those qualified to use them. This was felt to be undemocratic. A group of state-college presidents informed me that they wanted one of their own on the Council, and many of their own on our panels. They also wanted revised standards in their own special case, and annual quotas of our money. They were pretty much perfect examples of constituency politics: men of little mind, some character and much familiarity with legislatures. And they represented the alternative to my confirmation.

A *Washington Star* editorial appeared on the 18th of February, all fire and brimstone. It enraged Pell, who played the buffoon of the piece. His office called mine to break off diplomatic relations. One the other hand, Sid Yates called to say that it was just the right thing. The President sent my name up to the Senate just after this; it was clear that the battle would go public in a fairly noticeable way.

I began the week of the 23rd of February by calling on Senator Schweiker who was an *Adams Chronicle* fan and we spent some time talking over the confirmation. Then there was a call from the Majority Leader's office, telling me to show up right away. Mike Mansfield had never heard of the Adams grant, and knew nothing of NEH: in fact he asked me why I was in his office. I stumbled around for a moment or two, then described the Pell business. Mansfield said simply that there were other members of the committee, and that I better get around to seeing them all: the subtext evidently being that I was all-right with him. But it was an unnerving interview; Mansfield was famously vague and silent and I had to ask myself questions and then answer them.

On the 5th of February there was an authentic Great Moment in Government: John Barcroft, Director of the Endowment's Public Division, won the Arthur Fleming award for, among other things, the design of our State-Based program. Pell was at the moment trying to corrupt our legislation, divert our budget and deny my confirmation because of this program; and could not have been made to look more foolish intentionally.

The dance of courtesy began. Senator Williams was approached by more intermediaries. I got word from Jay Hall,a Council Member and lobbyist for General Motors that he had spoken to Jennings Randolph on my behalf. Randolph mattered a good deal—he was the senior Senator in office, and of course right at the top of the sub-committee. Randolph gave his word to support me, from which he never deviated.

There was a half-hour interview on the first of March with Senator Eagleton, interested but non-committal. Then a talk with Cranston, who again lied that he would support me. Senator Hathaway likewise; so that I had what appeared to be all the Republican votes and most of the Democratic ones. At this point, if everyone kept his word, Pell seemed outnumbered.

I had a very good talk with Senator Stevens of Alaska, who had taken over from Alan Bible on the appropriations committee. Our hearing came up on the 3rd of March, and Stevens ended it with the unnecessary but welcome remark that my work had been "outstanding." The *Star* emphasized that the next day; "outstanding" by now having come to be a kind of code phrase in Washington which indicated that all who used it lined up on my side. I wondered if Pell was going to ransack the dictionaries for another standard.

Then came the fateful talk with Harrison Williams on the fourth of March. He had evidently had his ears filled by Pell and could make nothing of the issues. He said that Pell told him we had "philosophical" differences, a new entrant in the vocabulary of this issue. By the end of the hour he was wearily shaking his head over what seemed to be pretty familiar behavior. He said that he would put his staff on the case and let me know. For all the assurances that he was sympathetic he didn't seem enthusiastic; or much interested. And at his level of seniority in the Senate the matter of NEH must have seemed like a buzzing mosquito.

The new legislation proposed by Pell appeared on the 10th of March; it was clearly designed to take out on the agency the resentment that I had raised. NEH was to be cut ten million dollars below NEA; and there were a variety of other provisions which seemed vindictive: cuts in our gift and matching allowance as well as in the total amount of money available and restrictions of other kinds. When Bob Kingston went up to see Biddle on the 12th of March he was told that the bill was "punitive," an attack on the agency because it was more vulnerable than its Chairman. It was an astonishing admission.

From now on authorization and confirmation would be tied in a Gordian knot, and most of Pell's energies would go towards crippling the agency.

The first of two meetings with Jack Javits took place on the 15th of March, prompted by the more incendiary provisions of Pell's bill. I went over the probable reaction of some of the most powerful and vocal cultural institutions in this country to a law that would cut their resources because its author could not get at me. Javits would be perceived as a willing co-author, and get more headaches over authorization than over the confirmation itself. He was quite furious, and determined to get the bill back to normal: among the things that aggravated him was the realization that the wreckage of our State-Based program would now make it possible for Nevada and Utah to get as much money as New York.

At that point all was hopeful, Pell having created his own opposition even among those connected to him. But by the end of the month Javits slipped away. We met again, and he said that Pell had refused to yield. In the light of that—and of his own close personal relationship to Pell—he could only advise me to wait until after the election. I pointed out that he had promised to help; and that he was after all the ranking Minority Member.

He sighed like a man familiar with moral dilemmas, and said that I should canvass the committee to see if one Democrat and one Republican would crash its agenda for me. Good advice, but the case had in effect been closed. The Senate runs by procedure, and there is no other way to get it to act. I would have to break that procedure now while Pell would be protected by it. There were a dozen members of the committee ready to vote for me, and perhaps one or two against: but they would never come to that vote unless the ranking minority Member forced it. I knew enough about Javits not to be surprised, and left in good order. But it was clear not that I had lost, although I would spend the next six months fighting as hard as possible.

A few days later Javits' aide said that there would be a new strategy, with the Senator pulling for me on the sidelines, but not officially in the fight. The scenario was to approach Schweiker and Jennings Randolph, and have them introduce my name before the committee. They would, if possible, break into the agenda of other business and request the committee to act.

The American Jewish Committee got into high gear, and made me the keynote speaker at its annual meeting in Washington. President Ford was the other main speaker, so that their feelings lost no emphasis. Hy Bookbinder hoped by this to draw Javits' attention to what his constituents thought.

April saw dozens of little things that may or may not have added up: Jay Hall and Bill Baroody went once more to Senator Randolph, and once more got his assurance that I had at least one Democratic vote on the committee. There was a phone call from O'Hare airport from Len Garment, who had just escaped from a forty-five minute interview with Pell in New York. Pell was determined not to have me as Chairman, but was still without a reason; he did say that the would write into the authorizing bill that no Chairman could be reappointed without having done an "extraordinary" job. He still threatened revelations that would ruin me, if the matter ever came to a hearing. I still invited him to state them. He still declined the opportunity.

In early May I had lunch with Don Rumsfeld at the Pentagon, on a mission very different from most of its business. He thought that Senator Hathaway, who aspired to naval installations in Maine, might be the right man to break the procedural knot.

In May Pell was defeated in committee over the State-Based amendment. Javits tried five or six forms of compromise, and came up with something pretty much like what he and I had thought would do. The House promised to sustain my position, so that Pell failed in his first great aim, which was to punish the agency because of me. Those present at the hearing said that it was pretty much a dead loss for him, and something of a humiliation; which was a great satisfaction to the small-minded, myself among them.

By early June the media had become much involved. There were articles and editorials, before all this was over, in *The New Republic, The Washington Post, The Washington Star, The New York Post, The New York Daily News, National Review, The Wall Street Journal* and many in between. George Will noted that the differences were both political and idiosyncratic:

> NEH offends some political sensitivities because it bestows benefits in a non-political way on the basis of merit. . . . Pell wants the money to go in block grants as a matter of right, not merit, to paid state agencies, appointed by governors. . . . Pell has wistfully but not wisely hoped that NEH would wind up supporting "lumberjacks" and "grocers" and "shoemakers." The arts endowment can do that: Anyone can dabble at watercolors, or weld car bumpers into something the arts endowment considers art. But NEH can hardly give a lumberjack $500 to dabble at, say, historical research.

Anne Crutcher's editorial in the *Star* was formidable, concentrating on the perversion of due process and the fact that everyone on the committee except Pell was ready to vote; and to approve the nomination. It hit Pell pretty hard, and for a while made me think force was counter-productive; but other members of the committee thought it accomplished its purpose.

The editorial did in fact prove to be the right medicine. A good friend of mine was called by Harrison Williams, now uncomfortable enough to be provoked into action. He was angry and frustrated by Pell, and had nothing particular against me. Williams was something of an old-time politician, and like everyone else except Pell wanted an arranged solution. But Pell insisted now that I was guilty of "elitism"—which had Senator Williams scratching his head and looking for a dictionary. At any rate he said the committee would meet to talk about a hearing. What a way to get the democratic process started.

Getting the committee to talk about the matter was like

milking a bull. I spent the next month in correspondence with Williams, trying to get him to eat his words. A basic pattern did seem to emerge: when Javits, Hathaway, Williams and others were first contacted they expressed doubt about Pell's seriousness, and surprise at his position. There was a high ratio of initial support for me, corroborated by contact with the press or local constituencies. But trade-offs and senatorial courtesy then silenced the other Democrats on the committee. They expressed private sympathy and said that if it ever came to a vote on the appointment, no matter what Pell wanted they would vote for me. *But if it came to a vote on whether or not to hold a hearing, they would have to vote against me.* It was literally a Catch–22: they would not allow a meeting to take place; but if it did, I could have their votes.

The legislation went well because of supernatural activity on the agency's part, and because the opposition could find so little to justify. The House continued to fight the Senate version of the bill; and Blanchette Rockefeller, a Council Member, successfully argued parity of the two agencies to Javits. Somewhat to my surprise, it looked as if none of the provisions in Pell's bill would ever become law; that all he had accomplished was to defeat himself in this matter while looking pretty bad at the same time.

Meanwhile, the stakhanovites never stopped work. Jay Hall kept on top of the business with Jennings Randolph, Arthur Krim phoned tirelessly on my behalf, Hy Bookbinder did everything but take the state of New Jersey apart in the effort to find something that would be an irresistible argument to Williams. There were even angry articles on my behalf in Pell's hometown paper, *The Providence Journal,* and Williams', *The Trenton Times.* It turned out that NEH was not invisible to the media.

A *Wall Street Journal* editorial appeared on the first of July, containing among other things an analogy between Pell and the inept Wayne Hays. Williams saw it, and was exercised. He gave a counter-statement to *The Trenton Times* saying that there would definitely be a hearing. A new administrative assistant took over Pell's office, and told my congressional man that

Pell's opposition was fathomless and not to be explained; and that he thought it about the silliest thing the Senator had ever done. The best thing, he thought, was for us to apply the same kind of pressure in Rhode Island that we had done nationally. It appears that Pell was encouraged by the relative quiet in his home state, although he was taking his lumps elsewhere. It was an excellent thought, and we heated up newspapers, constituents and contributors wherever they could be found.

The press had done an enormously effective job up to now; and I was grateful for its training-diet on Watergate. I would have been nowhere if it were not for the newspapers. Television ignored the matter; it was complex and not on their scale of public interest. Editorials and columns worked where nothing else would; and it was necessary to go outside of government in order to get government to function. In a way, my opposition had brought it on their own heads. Because Pell had so little to prove he fell in love with the idea of stating his reservations in a way that promised real disclosures, if not some scandal. By biting the ankles of the agency, however, he invited the opposition of the press. After his first argument was undone, that I was incapable and unsatisfactory, he went on to develop some favorite themes for them. The extent to which this backfired can be judged from *The Providence Journal*'s lead, "Pell Seeking To Bring Humanities To Mom and Pop Stores."

Nearly all the coverage was based on disgust with congressional procedures and Pell; but one piece, in the not very widely distributed *Washington International Arts Letter*, had some shrewd things to say about the side-effects of legislation. It began with the observation that Pell would attempt to have all nominations for the NEA and NEH councils subject to confirmation by the Senate. It sounded harmless, but would in fact involve even more politics than those forced on us by the White House Personnel Office. Not only would there be the normal attractions of patronage: Pell wanted labor to be "represented" on both Councils; which was simply to give the unions a chance actively to lobby for grants *within* the agencies. And Javits wanted someone from the fashion industry on the

Arts Council because he thought that fashion was part of the Arts, if not part of his constituency. Given the thrust of politics, there would be walloping benefits for an enterprise clearly commercial. Fashion in New York City and hobbies for the retired in Iowa were part of a new social definition: art, at least, was what people wanted to do when it was paid for by politics. As Agnes De Mille put it in the *Times*, "they're spreading it around geographically, like Kiwanis." The contours of a new definition for humanities were fairly plain.

On the 15th of June I met with Javits' aide, Greg Fusco, who was throughout honest and helpful. Fusco pointed out that it would be to my advantage to have action on the bill delayed until after confirmation. Pell would then not have the excuse that the appointment should be made only after the new bill had been passed, while, of course, doing everything possible to make passage of the bill impossible. Right then he was contentedly sending out two different messages to House and Senate: the latter understanding that he would be pleased to have a hearing after authorization; the former that he would never agree to anything on the conference agenda that was likely to let the bill go through. If his colleagues were to play ball with him, the nomination would lapse with the end of the congressional session.

But by the end of July both Javits and Williams had evidently had enough from friends, constituents, lobbyists, media, and everyone else on the case. They agreed to a hearing before the end of the session. Williams even made a little speech on the floor of the Senate guaranteeing a hearing—after the conference. Since the conference would by every indication take place at the very end of the congressional session there would be no time left to hold a hearing; and the nomination would lapse. Williams' speech had the effect of assuring everyone that the Senate would act while allowing it not to, which was a rather clever way of neutralizing my supporters.

The time-wasting began again. The American Jewish Committee sent off a rattling telegram to Williams stating what they thought of his maneuver. Once again the telephones were started, and all over the country academics put pen to hand again. *The New Republic* and the *Wall Street Journal* came out for me again, so that a little more light was on the matter than the committee wanted.

It was a pretty good week for the media; *Newsweek* spent a lot of time preparing coverage (never printed) which had the effect of galvanizing the committee. *The New York Daily News* pitched in with an editorial, and Pat Buchanan did a column. The conference committee actually met, and to most people's surprise, including my own, made progress on the bill. Activity became frantic, with friends on left and right drumming up the case, raging against the Senate in *New Republic* and *National Review* at the same time. The *Star* did a piece on the conference which sounded fine until one got to Pell's plan for picking up beer cans as part of the ideal humanities program.

As a result of the renewed press activity, a hearing materialized on the 15th of September, in the last days of the congressional session. Javits came out for re-appointment; but Pell, who chaired the proceedings, filibustered his way through the agenda for the last days of that session. Eventually the hearing ended with none of the issues resolved; with some passing allusions to grocers and lumberjacks; and with the expected victory of mind over natter. Although it was too late, the main purpose of a year's work had been served, to force a vote from the committee.

The count went along party lines, with only Jennings Randolph holding firm. Walter Mondale and Gaylord Nelson abstained. The committee was spared having to break ranks on their privilege: they only voted, 7 to 6, on whether or not to vote. All the Republicans and a majority of the Democrats informed Pell that if a vote on nomination itself were to take place it would go against him. Procedure allowed Pell to prevent that vote. In the opinion of the committee staff, this case had come as close as any in modern times to upsetting the practice of senatorial courtesy.

I met with Pell after the hearings, and he agreed that he would withdraw his opposition to me if Gerald Ford won the election.

CHAPTER XI

Art vs. The Arts

I have spoken of events until now, and perhaps ought to say something of ideas. This chapter and the two which follow it are concerned with certain definitions. And they are concerned not only with the National Endowment for the Humanities, but with its sister agency, The National Endowment for the Arts. The reason for this is twofold: I have unavoidably mentioned NEA many times in the text, and some things need to be said in clarification. And, of course, the two agencies make up a single if mythological institution: the National Foundation on the Arts and Humanities. It is not mythological, however, to suggest that the practice of the Arts Endowment, and its example, have heavily influenced both public and congressional understanding of the humanities..

Because the National Endowment for the Arts has such a good press, and because it serves such a large and conscious public it is often assumed that the Humanities Endowment also should be both visible and popular. And, it is often assumed that the work of the Humanities Endowment should be very like that of NEA: that is to say, it should constitute highly practical things which amuse, entertain, and benefit the public. But it may be useful momentarily to be theoretical, to question certain ideas and definitions about what art—or the arts—are, and what the humanities do.

I think it crucial to begin with the matter of defining art in order to understand the humanities. What, we may ask, is the position of art in our culture: why should it be supported and what does its support accomplish?

I think it a truism that art is now defined in terms of middle-class values and aspirations: it is the pursuit of the majority. Current dogma, selected almost at random from media or from publications of NEA assumes that art is quintessentially socially useful. And that dogma asserts that art should be universally accessible. It argues that distinctions of quality are invidious, a theme which makes possible the current relationship between art and politics. In the view of many who support government patronage, art serves a mass electorate. It provides "experience" and "activity" for that electorate.

But if art has become bourgeois, the artist has not. The artist thinks of himself as a political revolutionary. The function of his art is to express a position on public issues and to serve ideas. Also, to embody a particular kind of alienation, and to show that the aesthetic object is less important than the personality shaping it. The two sets of ideas are contradictory but not exclusive: the most established of museums will exhibit the blank canvas or empty frame which is a calculated insult to its own existence. By so doing, the institution exhibits its social responsibility (or responsiveness) and the artist his revolutionism. None of the values involved seems to have much to do with the practice of art.

The belief that art is a form of permanent revolution is probably as useless as the idea that it serves social values. In both cases the practice of art serves external ideas, and the object of art comes to represent something other than itself.

That art represents the General Will is a credo of public relations. But it is taken seriously enough, and has effects on artistic thought and activity which are serious enough to change their definition. One of the better sources for the argument that art is a public utility is the *Congressional Record*. Congressional debate on the National Endowment for the Arts has been conducted in a variety of moods since 1965, the year the Endowment was founded, but its common theme has been the public value of institutionalized creativity. Perhaps the most crucial of congressional debates were the authorization hearings held in both House and Senate in 1973, for it was then that support for the arts first decisively defeated its opposition. It was not a matter simply of the roll-call but of the thrust and conclusion of argument: here for the first time adherents of publicly supported art made a case which overwhelmed their opponents. That case was both ideological and political. To support federal patronage was no longer a matter of apologizing for high ideals. The tactics used were no longer those of smuggling in cultural support among other and higher proceedings. At this point in our cultural history a number of things, as in a chemical precipitation, became instantly plain.

Institutionalized art had by the seventies become economically important. That fact was indicated by the heavy representation of municipal lobbies in the wings. Perhaps more important, a cultural shift of major proportions had occurred. It was no longer necessary at hearings or on the floor of the House and Senate to defend art as a minority interest but as the vocation of a large and formidable constituency. Two other things were suggested by the tenor of congressional debate: that art had become identified with values previously confined to education or religion; and that art (or *the arts*, which are very different) had taken on bureaucratic shape and political identity.

In opening the debate in the House of Representatives, John Brademas invoked President Nixon's statement that the arts provided us with "the intangible but essential qualities of grace, beauty, and spiritual fulfillment." The interpretation of that rubric by Congress turned out to be a paradigm of a larger cultural process. On the floor of the House, Congressmen summarized countless arguments and affirmations provided by local and national lobbies for the arts. The main argument was that government should extend its social and educational programs, and that support of the arts and humanities was part of domestic support in general. Contingent arguments were intended to show that, so far as the arts were concerned, there was a direct connection between the appropriation of funds and the resolution of one or more social problems. And nothing could indicate better that art was a political commodity than the recognition that its support pleased important constituencies.

The argument for the support of the arts had little to do with the actual creation of aesthetic objects and even less with scholarship, criticism, or training. Art was what federal funds supported. Art assisted hospitals, urban ghettos, rural regions, community centers, and various agencies of welfare.

The social functions of art were emphasized in their variety, the debates suggesting that art displaced adolescent violence and anomie, encouraged craftsmanship, discouraged crime, and offered new opportunities for employment. Art was an alternative to drug addiction, an auxiliary to prison rehabilitation, and a solution to the problems of old age. Exposure to art might relieve inner-city tensions and possibly improve the tone of the adversary culture. Most appreciated of all was the effect of art—or the distribution of funds in its name—on regionalism. Hundreds of associations had sprung up under the influence of federal support of the arts, and they were necessarily connected to the economic life of congressional districts.

It was not mentioned but it was generally understood that these associations were composed of two new and important groups. The first was made up of traditional patrons of the arts, and of those who aspired to patronage. They had found that organization into public corporations relieved them of the personal responsibility to contribute funds while it maximized their influence on government policy. Since this group tended to be affluent, educated, and socially conscious, it was involved also in traditional political activities: the trustee of an association sponsoring the arts would typically have a previous connection with fund-raising. He would have experience and weight in civic affairs. But now, instead of taking on the burden of solicitation or of personal contribution, it was possible to exert leverage on the operations of government. To be a member of a State Council on the Arts was to receive substantial amounts of federal funds, and to have a voice in their distribution. Local sponsorship and patronage were extended into the mutual relationship of Congress and a constituency.

The second group was bureaucratic, composed of men and women who found new administrative careers created by the distribution of public funds. The expertise required is not entirely artistic: Dick Netzer, in *The Subsidized Muse*, states that lobbying for additional funds is a primary function of State

Council staffs. Both groups, the members and the staff, lobby in another sense, which is to identify the regional support of art with direct social service. As they define what they do, art takes on the shape of domestic assistance to selected constituencies.

During the debate, the language of congressional discourse concentrated on numbers and participation. "Thousands of people, and whole communities" were the object of federal subvention. It was consistently stated that the benefits of art were in fact social, and that their civic effect was nowhere better shown than in the diffusion of money and programs among the young, the disadvantaged, and minorities. The remarks of one Congressman which I have cited give an exceptionally useful sense of art as a social activity. It is a local service directed at an important constituency:

> Iowa has one of the highest percentages of population aged 65 or older. It is therefore particularly fitting that the Iowa Arts Council this year provided assistance to the Iowa State Commission on the Aging for a senior citizen arts festival, an event which proved highly successful and which I hope will be repeated yearly. We have an immense reservoir of training, experience, and talent in older Americans—upon retirement they have increased time to devote to these talents, to their crafts and hobbies. The federal, state, and local programs in the arts should take particular cognizance of their needs and their potentialities.

It was a representative statement; others claimed the same kind of benefit, and made the same assumptions about the ends and means of artistic activity and support.

Political discourse needs to be discounted because it always implies social benefits. But there are in speeches like the above two things that ought not to be explained away as the normal exaggeration of congressional salesmanship. The first is the tactical end of distributing funds to constituencies in the name of art. The second, less political, is more important: it is the redefinition of artistic activity. That redefinition was provided by the various lobbies for art upon which congressional committees rely almost absolutely. The bureaucracy of art—members and staff of State Councils, the National Endowment for the Arts, and House and Senate committees—believe that the primary purpose of the support of art is the distribution of funds. They believe in *programs* rather than *grants*. A grant is specifically designed to produce a particular effect; a program means only to be an instrument of equity. Most people prefer programs, because stipulated amounts annually are conveyed to all interested parties, which eliminates application, competition, and uncertainty.

The debates summed up issues connected not only to the support of art but to its practice and definition. The language of social piety tends to disguise a profound problem of interpretation. It is plain that artistic activity is no longer thought of as professional activity. It has in fact become the opposite, a form of middle-class relaxation. The "democratic" assumption is that we are all artists, while the populist assumption underlying it is that activity is its own end. This has a superficial resemblance to the Victorian idea that art exists for its own sake, but is very different. The implication of activity being its own end is that standards are superfluous: art is anything with creative intentions.

I think that at least part of the new definition of art becomes clear through its new political identity. It is indispensable to begin consideration of that identity with the difference between *art* and a term that has come to displace it, "the arts." *Art* means creativity and refers itself to the history of achieved things from Altamira to the present. "The arts," a phrase which has become an essential part of the vocabulary of policy, is used generally to imply creativity while promoting the ideas of the congressional debate that I have described, and the subsidy of associations, bureaucracies, and institutions. It means the distribution of funds for purposes *felt* to be artistic.

Some of the most praiseworthy efforts of the National Endowment for the Arts have gone into the maintenance of institutions. But a certain moral—and artistic—cost has been involved. I am not speaking simply of the diversion of funds for lobbying or other aspects of political reality. In the fourteen years since the inception of this agency, and after the expenditure of the better part of a billion dollars, *we are hard put to name a single work of art worth recollecting that it has made possible*. Nor can we associate its support with a productive idea affecting the understanding of art either by artists or their audience.

The NEA represents "the arts" rather than art, which is understandable given the fact that it reflects the will of its constituency. And "the arts" stand for the distribution of funds rather than specific accomplishments; the subsidy of associations promoting themselves as well as their purposes; the relationship of the private sector of patronage to government; the use of art for social purposes; the satisfaction of particular constituencies.

Those constituencies are larger than one might think. There are 25,000 members of Actor's Equity and about 15,000 amateur theaters. The Bureau of the Census states that there are now about a million people who identify themselves as artists by occupation. Artistic identity is having something of a boom. Without being simplistic, one can say that is probably because many vocations, like teaching, have been devalued; especially those dealing with cultural affairs. Competing institutions of culture have declined—religion, for example. And, as social status has become a matter of self-ascription, artistic *character* has become enormously popular. The use of the phrase "creative" has changed in an interesting way: it has been removed from the realm of achievement and applied to another realm entirely. What it means now is an attitude about the self; and it belongs not to aesthetics but to pop psychology.

There has been a natural overflow from the promotion of "the arts." More or less without a stop we are informed by the new class of government patrons that art is a universal good. One of the few activities of government not criticized by the media is its cultural subvention. And, of course, the availability of funds always draws into existence those able to benefit from them.

Yet actual creativity is hard to find. I have asked a deputy chairman of the National Endowment for the Arts why that agency risked so much resentment by refusing to give more than 2 or 3 percent of its annual budget to individual artists. This policy has made it easy to attack NEA for its subservience to institutions, and for its plodding subsidy of production and performance. The reply was that there are not enough good artists in the United States to justify giving them more than 3 percent of NEA's annual funds. The million citizens characterizing themselves as artists for the census—joined by many more than a million to whom the arts are less than a vocation but more than a diversion—have creative intentions. But they cannot paint.

The politics of "the arts" is clearly a cycle: funds are distributed to organizations created by the distribution of funds. Netzer's *The Subsidized Muse*, which is the best study of the economics of government patronage, states flatly that State Arts Councils "may be regarded as costly sops for Congressmen determined to spread federal largesse widely and thinly, and as a means of creating a nationwide corps of lobbyists for NEA." There are of course other social purposes: in a piece in *Commentary*, Samuel Lipman observed that "arts funding is seen by politically and socially activist groups as providing the means of increased visibility for their causes." Other benefits have been the prestige conferred by artistic purpose; significant numbers of administrative jobs; and the connection more firmly established between the arts and good causes.

Support of the social theory of art derives not from the congressional imagination but from the influences shaping it. If art means middle-class associations like State Councils, and ceaseless promotion of activity, then Congress will support that. If art means the diversion of funds to the young, the old, or minorities, then Congress will find that too acceptable. The arts constituency determines finally what the definition of art or of "the arts" will be. And that constituency has in the most determined way exempted artistic activity from critical standards. Art is whatever is done, whether crafts, hobbies, or simply the display of intentions. It is an ennobled form of middle-class entertainment.

Modern art has long been noted for the strenuous attempts of artists to offend the bourgeois imagination. But art now behaves as if it were anything but the culmination of the modernist movement. It is a radical product consumed by a distinctly un-radical class. An enormous amount of artistic activity has now been concentrated into performance, production, and other middle-class modes. The models are the Kennedy Center and Wolf Trap Farm, large establishments heavily supported by government, corporations, and foundations, and offering a combination of mass-audience programs and enough adversary culture to stay ahead of the media. The sixties may have been radicalized art and its discourse, but the seventies and eighties have given it back to the middle class. It is difficult to talk about contemporary art as if it still had anything to do with modernism. Music, drama, dance, and exhibition are now the major modes, while the art of ideas matters far less than it used to. Poetry, for example, is now limited to the academic audience, although in the earlier part of the century it had a much more formative role. The performing arts now dominate and they represent the new role of social art: an auxiliary to daily life provided by the mutual operations of large institutions.

It makes no sense to be ungrateful for performance and production, or for the fortunate survival of civic benevolence. But subsidized events for large audiences tend inevitably to become a kind of cultural welfare. They are designed for the largest common denominator, and frequently translate art into another idiom.

The nervous attitude of art critics toward corporate support of performance is based upon suspicion of the profit motive. There is no denying that the sponsors of mass-audience culture have their own interests in mind. Texaco has stated that its support of the Metropolitan Opera broadcasts is based upon economic facts: the opera audience is loyal and buys Texaco products; a significant proportion of the 400,000 shareholders in the company own stock because of their interest in its cultural activities; the opera audience is "upscale" or composed of those with discretionary income; and the audience is politically sophisticated, receptive to the corporation's side of controversy involving energy, taxation, and regulation. But it is a truism that sponsorship is a matter of self-interest. What is more significant is the relationship between corporate and public and public ideas about culture.

The most interesting thing about corporate support for the arts is not the profit motive but something that might be called the cultural imperative. A survey of corporate backing of the performing arts in *Advertising Age* claims that "corporate involvement in social, civic, and cultural activities" is now routine. That support is not related directly to sales; corporations too have visions of social mobility, and derive the same benefits from patronage as traditionally accrue to individuals.

Corporations have perforce a sense of their place in society, and within culture. As we frequently see in televised commercials, corporations no longer exclusively try to make sales. They present interminable displays of their social conscience; of the love and loyalty and services they live to confer. The usual perception is that corporations are trying to sell themselves instead of a product. But even that is not really accurate. Corporations may be trying to sell themselves—and to buy respect—but they are even more insistently trying to articulate what they believe are common values. Their nervous affirmations of clean water for good fishing or new forests for the next generation rest on the understanding that democratic institutions are involuntary social arbiters. If they do not affirm certain ideas they may be accused of opposing them. Corporations undertake to support whatever ideas are popular, vaguely moral, and untroublesome. They may even believe some of these ideas. They can certainly interpret the *Zeitgeist* as well as art critics.

It is necessary to observe, if only parenthetically, that corporations are now at the stage of structural development implying cultural support on a large scale. They employ many people in offices of public affairs which are subordinated to ideas about public relations. There is a good deal of ready money available because the tax code exempts 5 percent of profits for charitable donations. Corporations have come to resemble State Councils on the Arts, maintaining bureaucracies devoted to the distribution of tax-free funds. They are vulnerable to local pressures, especially in metropolitan areas: corporate officers maintain the same position, and must perform the same largesse, as entrepreneurs did before them. But they can only live up to social expectations by dispensing tax-free corporate donations.

The managerial class has the same mind-set as those who define cultural values in utilitarian terms. Art as a diffuse social activity fits the corporate idea about its own place in democratic society. That kind of art is universal and uncontroversial. It begins with a head start since intellectuals and the media find it difficult to quarrel with support of "the arts." There are more than political benefits, for executives are assured that they exist culturally. In an age in which cultural issues matter as much as political issues, that is an advantage.

There is an especially revealing passage in the survey of *Advertising Age*:

> There is no doubt, as former CBS president Frank Stanton pointed out to the 25th anniversary conference of the Public Relations Society of America, that the essential values of the public "are most clearly evident, and in some instances evident only, in the arts—in music, the drama, and the dance, in the architecture and design and in the literature of the people and of the times."

When critics of corporate patronage hunt for the profit motive they overlook what Stanton calls "values" and what others have described, according to *Advertising Age*, as the "community" or even the "communion" that the corporation pursues with its customs. The corporation goes so far as to hope for "involvement with a customer as a total human being"—which is somewhere, one supposes, between a theological and a matrimonial relationship. The corporation believes, probably rightly, that the educated middle class has a morally positivist understanding of culture. Art, in that understanding, reflects the orderliness and intelligibility of life. It celebrates social beliefs and reinforces individual self-esteem. And, since it is just about the only aspect of industrial democratic life to have retained ritualistic, mystical, and even holy elements in its character, it is beyond criticism.

Performance is seen by its sponsors as an occasion of social solidarity. It is superego art. We can never be sufficiently reminded that it brings people together, is accessible to every mind and sensibility, has moral and therapeutic benefits, and implies the common taste of a mass middle class.

Within the social definition of "the arts," distinctions are invidious: Warhol matters so long as he is a celebrity; the same can be said of Rubens. Not since the happy ending of *King Lear*, provided by Nahum Tate for the Enlightenment, has the interest of the audience been so solicited. The age of reason preferred a world without tragedy—and so it got philosophy. At the end of Tate's version of *King Lear*, Kent, Gloucester, and the king retire to a monastery while Edgar marries Cordelia. It is a triumph of poetic justice. The implications for us are fairly clear. When production and performance are tailored to a theory of what the public taste demands, good art will not necessarily be rejected, but bad art will certainly become accepted.

The consumption of bad art has been made easier by its sponsors, its production by other factors. There have been a number of theories for artistic decline, especially in painting. The most visible attack on painting recently has been Tom Wolfe's *The Painted Word*, and in that book the blame is put pretty squarely on the devil's work done by criticism. In Wolfe's view—and although the book is outrageously funny, its message is serious—movements or mini-movements like Op and Pop art follow the temptations of ideas. An idea is broached by a critic, and a market created on the spot as artists try to embody it, sell it, and live up to its philosophy. But if anything, the critics of contemporary art (like those of the movies) seem to be better than their material. It is not that ideas are bad, but that contemporary art seems to be dominated by ideas which are second-rate. It might even be said of much of our art that it works without ideas; that it has become technique without a motive.

One of the most interesting of cultural facts to be recognized by government is the separation of art not only from a theory but from the discourse of other disciplines. In splitting its patronage between arts and humanities, the federal government has acknowledged the preferences of opposed constituencies. One Endowment deals with books and ideas, with scholarship and research, with the theory and criticism of art—and that is the Humanities Endowment. The Arts Endowment deals only with what is left. What is left includes a good deal, about twenty different activities from dance to folk crafts. It ranges from the subsidy of the housewife who played the piccolo in Leadville, Colorado, immortalized by a House Committee on Appropriations as the ultimate object of federal patronage, to the subsidy of the Metropolitan Opera. But what is left needs to be measured against what has been left out.

At least in government, which is not a bad indicator of social preference, the disciplines of thought have been removed from those of "activity." The arts are perceived—and legislatively defined—as the realm of "experience" or of sensation; as a form of entertainment; and as a diffuse activity which is its own end. Government is sometimes all too good an indicator: it reflects in this case the separation of art from sustaining thought, a separation as important as that which has been discerned between science and its opposing cultures.

Within the world of art itself there has been a separation of word and act. Scholarship takes place in universities and deals with the dead. The criticism of art takes place in the media, and is practiced there by those who believe that art and its social context are identical. If there is a universal theme to media coverage of the arts it is that the amount of money distributed to constituencies, institutions, and approved social causes defines ideal "support." As for the practice of the arts, that has become our largest amateur activity.

For about a century and a half the professional artist has viewed himself (sometimes rightly) as untutored genius, social critic, political savant, existential philosopher, and in half-a-dozen other roles. These have set him off from the rest of bourgeois society and made him its greatest critic. But the quality of enabling ideas has fallen off since Shelley said that poets were the unacknowledged legislators of mankind. Modernism arose, in part, because of artistic hostility to bourgeois values and because of the hostility of those values to art. But the world depicted in the novels of Sinclair Lewis no longer exists. The middle class has long since put up the white flag and embraced the creed of its conquerors. Art is the most honored of all civic activities, and "creativity" is the most honored of all motivations.

The desire of modernism to offend the middle class was subordinate to the production of work which meant more, and contained more, than the reflection of what it hated. Oscar Wilde wrote that only bad artists had ideas or "character": the good ones "exist simply in what they make, and consequently are perfectly uninteresting in what they are." The moral for us is somewhat ambiguous, for it suggests that artists express feelings about bourgeois society in lieu of actual creativity. By now artistic alienation should have run its course, like all other inspirations. But our world is still being addressed by art as if it were Victorian; either the sins of the father are being visited upon the third generation, or those of the artist upon his audience.

The visual and dramatic arts have in the last two decades accomplished something self-defeating. They reflect social ends and political arguments so perfectly as to become what they represent. It has been often observed that Dickens invented some of the most stupendous bores in literature. But his description of them was never boring. In fact, his bores are fascinating. The paradox of art is that it must recognize some difference between the model and the work. If it didn't, then there would not need to be any work, only a model. By refusing to distance itself or complete an act of interpretation, art becomes what it loathes. If it remains a pilot-fish of the bourgeoisie, then its movements are restricted to the path of the beast it feeds on.

Resentment, ugliness, and absurdity are major motifs of contemporary art. But it is after all self-defeating for painting and drama to have become resentful, ugly, and absurd.

Jacques Barzun in *The Use and Abuse of Art* describes the exhibition of works molded in human excrement; the artist who exhibited himself, framed by plastic testicles, as he reclined in a coffin; and a third who "cut off pieces of his own flesh and photographed them." Daniel Bell in *The Cultural Contradictions of Capitalism* describes the transformation of drama from rhetorical to visual art:

> In the "Destruction of Art" symposium held in the Judson Church in New York in 1968, one of the participants suspended a live white chicken from the ceiling, swung it back and forth, and then snipped off its head with a pair of hedge-clippers. He then placed the severed head between his legs, inside his unzippered fly, and proceeded to hammer the insides of a piano with the carcass. At the Cinémathèque in 1968, the German artist Herman Nitsch disemboweled a sheep onstage, poured the entrails and blood over a young girl, and nailed the carcass of the animal to a cross.

Aristotle, who saw a good deal of drama, and said that spectacle was the weakest part of performance, evidently didn't know the half of it.

The late Harold Rosenberg wrote of the German arts festival Documenta 5 that it was momentarily captivated by the current prestige of mental illness. Since madness has been adopted by therapy as a more authentic condition than sanity that has become a recurrent theme in painting. The theme of "self-expression" at Documenta 5took the idea of the self to be that of pop psychology, i.e., a dramatization of ascribed feelings:

> Genuine schizophrenia shaded off into "artistic" or drug-induced imitations in galleries of photographic horrors involving fish heads, genitalia, evisceration, blood-

> stained religious vestments, and crude crucifixes, plus photographic portraits of the artist gagged, gashed, and split in two.

Art shares in the general illiteracy of intellectuals, and ideas generated by the social disciplines articulate its resentment. To some extent the motives are political: not simply to attack bourgeois taste but to reject and devalue those standards which imply the existence of a legitimate social order. But there is a particular vulnerability in the visual arts that cannot be explained entirely in terms of political beliefs or social resentment.

The explosion of cultural criticism from Ezra Pound to Lionel Trilling left the visual arts untouched. But the effects on the arts of literacy were profound. Malraux suggests in *The Voices of Silence* that the paintings of the past three centuries cannot compare with what was done before that time; and it might be said, with less exaggeration, that nothing before 1920 can compare with the criticism after it. The number of poets in that period who were intellectually significant for culture at large as well as within their vocation was extremely large. That number included Pound, Eliot, John Crowe Ransom, Robert Penn Warren, and Robert Lowell. As men of letters their only competition can come from the greatest of the Romantic poets. Poetry either resisted ideology, as in the case of W. H. Auden, or transcended it.

From 1920 on it has been characteristic that critics like Trilling could work in fiction, and that poets like Auden could master criticism. But the visual arts, and too much of drama, have separated out from the unified movement of modernism, and treated technique and politics as if they were ideas.

The story of the arts is that of two decades. Painters were in the thirties no more inherently vulnerable to the Popular Front than were poets or novelists, but they did not resist it as well. They were bemused by the high status of official culture under Communism, and have indeed never recovered from the attractions of that notion. Artists became identified with the cause, and art was understood to be a technique expressing political belief. Writers had begun to circulate nationally, to infiltrate universities, and to work out their independence, but artists concentrated into a single and much smaller society in which it was difficult to be different. There were no Orwells in the visual arts.

The sixties completed what the thirties had begun. The political failure of radicalism led it to a sustained and successful attack on the cultural realm. There was a cross-fertilization of political righteousness and "creativity." It was in the sixties that radicalism confused its style with its accomplishment, and artists confused themselves with the work of art. And, of course, a lot of people confused themselves with artists.

It has been said that modernism contained the seeds of its own destruction, which seems probable enough. But the definition of art as a political ideology or a social attitude was a product not of modernism but of the sixties. The modernists attacked the middle class because art stood for values which the latter seemed not to understand; the burgeoning of artists who hate art derives from other motives. If, as *Advertising Age* reminds us, even corporations realize that "the essential values of the public" are "most clearly evident, and in some cases evident only," in art, then the war on aesthetics becomes politically understandable.

In defense of the artist's resentment of art the claim is routinely made that freedom finally does imply an end not only to objective standards, but to moral or imaginative constraints. Perhaps. But Harold Rosenberg describes an instance which puts that conclusion in some doubt. Jean Toche, who defines his own artistic genre as the composition of manifestoes and protests, has accused the Museum of Modern Art of vandalism because it removed an inscription spray-painted by another "artist" on the *Guernica* of Picasso. Toche was supported in this gesture by over a hundred teachers, critics, and curators who denounced the museum. Which leads one to reflect that it may be difficult to decide what is the *Mona Lisa* of this art form, the sledge-hammering of the *Pietá* or the explosion of the Parthenon.

Unfortunately for all of us, the visual arts insist on defining themselves in terms which are derivative. Giant excavations or earthworks become a "statement" about the landscape; miles of white sheets strung across the countryside imply the "labor" of all involved in the enterprise. With every step that art takes toward "dialogue" with the times, it moves closer to a position abandoned with great indignation more than a century ago. "Dialogue" is, after all, a kind of synonym for the "communion" which the corporation seeks so passionately and so advisedly with its clientele. It makes no difference that it is recommended to us by the current avant-garde. As a matter of fact, in *Artculture*, Douglas Davis reviews the moribund argument that the "dialogue" of artist and society is essential. We are back to the idea, already old in Plato's *Republic* and even there unconvincing, that art ought to be socially responsible. Its new responsibility is predictable: "The 70's" Davis said, "are a decade in which appalling truths have finally become clear to large masses of people, from the poisonous quality of the air we breathe to the stupendous revelations of corruption that accompanied Nixon's resignation." The function of art is said to be to interpret those truths to us. That seems to be exactly what modernism was trying to kill off when it declared its social independence. By labyrinthine ways a century of frantic contemporaneity has found itself back to square one. The artist thinks of himself as a revolutionary, but addresses himself to approved social truths. The business of painting is, evidently, to hate Nixon.

Government has defined the arts as non-intellectual activity for the majority. Sponsors from the private sector think of art as a repository for social values. And artists are guided by ideas or sub-ideas which fit rather nicely alongside these definitions. It is not only that a common danger is posed by the attack on quality and standards: government betraying its impatience with any obstacle to majority participation, and artists asserting that standards are relics of a dead past. The sum of attitudes from opposing sides is that art has no particular value in itself.

CHAPTER XII

The Public Interest

The central question confronting the two Endowments has to do with the public interest. It has two parts: how do they define their work? and what effect is it to produce? If their work is to be thought of as an inexplicable benefit conferred on large masses of voters then clearly one should worry only about the sums of money conveyed and the amounts of satisfaction experienced. We have come perilously close to the statement and acceptance of that interpretation in the operation of the National Endowment for the Arts. One hopes that will not eventually be said of the National Endowment for the Humanities.

Identifying a problem or an interest is not especially difficult; pursuing a solution is. And of course even identification can be difficult, at least for agencies not equipped for the job. Few of us would trust the Department of Education to state the criteria of a good and useful education; the same number would mistrust the efforts of the National Endowment for the Arts to identify in good faith the characteristics of excellent art. Both agencies of government would in any case almost certainly give us the same answer: that good art and good education were things enabling us to live together more sociably. That is to say, from the beginning, it is unlikely that political agencies would care to risk definition, since that excludes, and comparison, since that is politically invidious.

The situation of the National Endowment for the Arts is like that of any other agency. Not only does it have a limited amount of funds to disburse; it must face the unpleasant fact that the huge constituency it attempts to arouse in order to increase its appropriations wishes to absorb them. One paradox of bureaucratic life is that such a large audience must be generated; must write to Senators and Representatives; organize in lobbies and associations; have itself legitimized by media—and that it will then turn into an adversary. Hence the conscious separations: identifying the public interest and not pursuing it. The public interest may demand some change in some condition. But it is far easier to satisfy a *constituency*. And, those who combine themselves into a constituency for subsidized art in America often become recipients of funds; this tends to soften their critical judgements.

It goes without much saying that allotment of funds toward the pursuit of a problem means to the media that the problem is being satisfactorily addressed.

What are some of the advantages of identifying and not pursuing an interest? To take an example not entirely hypothetical, let us say that the Endowment for the Arts has discerned insufficient numbers of good paintings currently made in the United States. The Endowment knows perfectly well most of the reasons for this: there are few good schools of painting; there are few meaningful competitions for painters; there are few professional standards visible. If it is in the public interest to have more good paintings, then it is clearly desirable to train better artists, and train artists better. Perhaps—since the NEA compares itself routinely to the spirit of the Renaissance—we should introduce competitions like those for the gates of the Baptistry in Florence or the design of Saint Peter's. Perhaps higher standards should be asserted by NEA, with the view of distinguishing between hobbies, arts, crafts, and, more in the spirit of the Renaissance, actual paintings. These are all possibilities.

But it would in fact be scandalous if some of the things I have suggested were to take place. All kinds of problems would be raised about equality. One would be the interference with distributive funding by sex, race or region. Another would be infringement of the belief that standards are discriminatory. Money would have to be withdrawn from congressional districts. Reasons would have to be adduced about the connection between identifying and pursuing the public interest. It would have to be widely understood that the pursuit of that interest often impedes general satisfaction—and decreases everyone's guaranteed annuity. Worst of all, the pursuit of such a specific interest as raising the quality of American painting would conflict with the unstated dogma that all demands for support are legitimate.

From the viewpoint of the agency, the best thing to be done under such circumstances is to claim that the distribution of funds to good causes—for inner city children, for women, for the aged, for minorities, for benevolent associations—is in fact the mode of pursuit for our comparability with the Renaissance. There will not be much disagreement. Congress will be enormously pleased by the social emphasis. The constituency will find that money is channelled to it on a regular basis in the name of both moral and artistic purposes. The media will see evidence of governmental activity. More people will be pleased by the disparity between identifying and pursuing the public interest than by the establishment of any connection.

The most common way that the National Endowment for the Arts has of defining the "public interest" is to refuse to endow the phrase with specific, hence restrictive meaning. In fact, under no matter which administration over the past fifteen years the NEA has made many allusions to public benefits, but almost none to a specific interest or set of interests served by the support of art. That is to say, it has not mentioned those things which it is *not* in the public interest to support. It has not identified institutions which are necessary to develop. It frequently alludes to things like the Viennese State Opera and suggests that if but enough funds were authorized, this country too could have such a company. But it never suggests that, no matter what amount of money is ever liable to be appropriated there is a conflict between the distribution of funds to every claimant, and the concentration of funds on a few strategic resources. In short, it argues that the public interest would best be followed simply by extending the services it now performs.

It is exceptionally difficult to get the National Endowment for the Arts to state the public interest in terms of distinctions to be made; of levels of quality to be attained; of kinds of standards to be imposed; of beneficiaries to be excluded. It is impossible to get the NEA to state the ends of support for the various arts in terms other than satisfaction of constituents. But it is not at all difficult to get the NEA to state the public interest in terms of benefits distributed.

In part this is due to congressional bias, and in part to the will to serve that bias. An interchange from joint hearings on authorization of 1973 may clarify this:

> Mr. Quie. The only question I have, again looking at those little designs up there and on the previous map, it seems like they are congregated along the east coast from Washington up to Boston. I know there are a lot of people up there, but there are a lot of people in California, too, and quite a number of people in between. Is there some reason why they tend to be congregated?

That is one of the least innocent questions imaginable. Al Quie—who was, incidentally, a strong supporter of both Arts and Humanities necessarily was interested in insisting that the money go, as he delicately put it, "in between"—perhaps to the state of Minnesota which he recently has graced as Governor. The question was put not because he did not know the answer, but because it indicated a boundary which the agency was being challenged to cross.

The blankness of NEA in regard to quantifying the public interest, or distinguishing between what is or is not the public interest, leads to some further problems. For example, much of the media coverage of the agency suggests that its failure are the result of *deviations*. Every now and then NEA will find itself compromised by nepotism. It will give grants to those who do not need them for purposes which no responsible critic or watchdog Congressman will want to see made. It will urge support for projects to put Bottlenosed Dolphins into Grand Opera, or to sprinkle paint from Haley, Idaho to Cody, Wyoming in order to commemorate the births of Ezra Pound and Jackson Pollack. Of course in their crazy way, even these indicate that democracy has charms.

But there is the possibility that such failures arise from the conscientious adherence to ideas and norms; that they proceed from a certain interpretation of what the public interest may be. In that case, those who wish to inkdrop the Western landmass or hang dry wash across the Colorado River may be representative figures, not eccentric exceptions. They may summarize the aims of an institution in a completely unselfconscious way. To dismiss them as embarrassments; to grant the occasional Golden Fleece Award may be precisely to confuse the issue. As Chesterton said of the evils in the novels of Charles Dickens, they seem to come not from our disorder but from our order itself.

Such proposals are bound to be received, and often to be recommended for funding by NEA. That is because of its interpretation of the "arts" themselves. As the agency reads this phrase it means the universal activities of constituencies. NEA understands those activities in these three ways. First, that all demands for support are legitimate demands. The dolphin and inkdrop projects are perhaps extreme forms that such demands will take, but they are representative forms. That is, they indicate that the definition of art and the purpose of support depend largely on the imagination of the proposer. The extraordinary multiplication of references to the Vienna State Opera by defenders of the NEA budget must be one of the best political jokes of the century because the only way that such a project can be funded is by concentrating funds and by depriving other projects of them. But the entire thrust of NEA policy is that every project has equal merit. There can be no opposition more complete than that between a Vienna State Opera and a system geared for the distribution of funds to all comers.

Second, standards may not be propagated because art is relative. In the ultimate sense this may be true: fragments of anonymous Cretan pottery belong in the Louvre along with Winged victory. Art can be literally *trouvé.* but finding that driftwood is art is different from believing that everything is. Or the obverse, which is that is is impossible to distinguish between what is art and what isn't. The latter is a viewpoint defended by NEA and sometimes by art departments at various universities. Of course it has the advantage of opening our eyes to the artistry of Nature, or artisanship, even of accident. It has the disadvantage of supposing that differences don't matter. As an ideology this form of relativism seems to tell the booboisie that it has no right to see its own self-vision imposed upon a universe of things and essences which are naturally socialist in their arrangement. As a political convenience, this obviates one of the most annoying of political problems, that of distinguishing between rival claims for money. Because of that, there may be no anterior distinction about the quality of art.

One kind of objective reading takes art to be the product of competing viewpoints, and the expression of superior talent. The reading I suspect NEA makes is that art is the expression of those with equal rights to be appreciated. And it is of course in that lexicon the expression of collectivities. Hence the third point, on morality. I have noted that art is, so far as government is concerned, good for society; instrumental in discouraging adolescent violence, displacing anomie, reducing crime, creating jobs, relieving the difficulties of old age, poverty and imprisonment, and bringing culture to ghettoes and to farms. The object being relentlessly social; to identify groups disadvantaged by age, sex, race, money and location, and to pursue their artistic interests. This brings up one of the paradoxes of our situation: that although the artist is supposed to be rebellious, outside the middle-class system of politics—engaged even in the undermining of that system—what he does is good for us. That in fact is the sole explanation for so much adversary art of the recent past. The strange thing, however, is not so much the bourgeois appetite for being insulted but the way in which adversary art is interpreted. It is against most conventional values but at the same time it uplifts us, changes our minds, influences our ideas: in short, exposing ourselves to it we become more tolerant, wiser, even better persons. Perhaps that is only half the paradox. The other half is that quite a lot of genuine art really *is* poised against conventional values. The work, like *Ulysses*, and the life, like the life of Joyce, is a real expression of distance, even of contempt. And to this we might add the work of Pound, of Flaubert, of the founders of modernism. Work really alienated from social illusions does not pretend to be redemptive. It is content to be what it is; it does not wish to make us better. And to that extent, it is free of hypocrisy.

The function of the arts as seen by the NEA (stated in the 1980 *Annual Report*) is to affect a large public which would otherwise remain morally inert. We are invited by that report to value *Walden* because Gandhi was influenced by it and India consequently liberated. The book is validated by the masses of the Third World. *Uncle Tom's Cabin* is according to this report a great example of literature deserving support because of the enthusiasm it generated for a good cause. But that is an insane kind of literary criticism: what would have happened to the book's reputation if the North had lost? In any case, questions of non-moral literary meaning are not addressed in this publication. What matters is not the art but the cause.

The function of support is approached in many ways by this *Annual Report*. It may be to honor many cultures, to be "multiracial," or even to fight against the restraints implied by obsolescent taste for Shakespeare, Beethoven and Mozart. Ultimately, that function is to remember that "there are millions of people whose lives can be enriched by the arts". What this means, of course, is that *effects* are everything. Art matters because it makes us less traditional, more liberal, more pleased with ourselves. But what art may itself be is not an issue. The Endowment prefers not to think that poetry makes nothing happen: it wants us, or at least Congress, to know that art makes us better. And it makes us better in a particular way, by sharing the ideas of Gandhi or Harriet Beecher Stowe. Art becomes a representation of liberal political impulses.

This is literary theory of a kind exemplified by Archibald MacLeish, who often wrote that Eliot and Pound were not major figures because their ideas were unkind. "Even the best of us," MacLeish wrote towards the end of his life, can only see "what we love." To write out of other feelings, as presumably, Dante, Swift and Eliot did, is to fail greatness. Such ideas exemplified on every prose page of the *Annual Report* give one the sensation of drowning in marshmallows.

When a federal agency like NEA interprets the arts it is morally selective. It tells us that art is educational; a kind of constructive criticism. It assures us on all public occasions that art brings people closer together. It does not suggest that there really is a world out there in which Rimbaud, Baudelaire, Flaubert, Hemingway, Joyce, Proust and Pound offer irreducible opposition to such assumptions. It does not tell us that art may be morally unassimilable. So that, in my view, the capacity of such an agency to pursue the public interest with respect to the arts will be seriously hampered by its interpretation of what art itself may be. I think that such an agency will always be tempted to perceive in art only what is useful in attracting mass political support. It will suggest that our museums are full of the work of dedicated builders, men and women whose moral, social and political viewpoint, while sometimes excessive or over-emotional, was really an elevated form of our own. In that respect the work of a federal agency in a democracy will bear uncomfortably close relationship to that of a ministry of culture whose primary mission is to support government.

I do not mean by this that grants are given to politically favored candidates. That may happen, but it happens only occasionally. On the contrary, grants are given to culturally favored candidates. The definition of art has come to include moral intention and those who argue that their proposal does social good become the most authentic candidates for support.

My own experience suggests some alternative interpretations of the terms in question. Most federal agencies, even those as small as the Arts and the Humanities Endowments, have attached to them a General Counsel's office. One assumes that agencies are involved in lawsuits and need legal advice. But there are few lawsuits, and the office is used in other ways. One reason for its existence is to redefine the mission of the agency. This office, following the lead of the Chairman sees how undesired things can be avoided and desired things included in the agency's activities. It is revealing to compare the description of an agency's activities with the idea of its mission described in authorizing legislation. Policy is the will of the administration of any agency as opposed to the limits set upon it. Tactically, it is the interpretation of all activities not covered by authorization. Of course it is also to be understood as carrying out the legislative intents; and in that too there is maneuvering room. But the essential thing for policy is how an agency maneuvers in, so to speak, empty space; how it defines what it does on its own.

It is hard to exaggerate the importance of this understanding of policy. Nowhere is it stated in the legislation of the National Endowment for the Arts that money is to be given for moral reasons, or that all art is relative in value. To that extent we can be hopeful about future possibilities. But that also implies the extent of the present difficulty: if Congress and the White House have not made prior decisions about the value or morality of art, if limits of interpretation have not been set, then present policies are doubly to be damned. We seem to reward bad art and amateur art and mass art not because we have to but because we want to.

When NEA discovered around 1970 that Congress was eager to distribute social benefits in the form of support of the arts it readily complied. It did not reserve space for maneuver. It simply accepted that art was a social benefit which could be distributed equitably. So that there was no productive argument with Congress over the logic of regional distribution of funds or parity within congressional districts. The opportunity to compromise with Congress was lost.

Even now the legislation governing the agency makes no explicit provision for social benefits. Public Law 89–209, as amended through 1980, says that the Chairman of the agency shall fund projects of artistic and cultural significance, those which meet professional standards, those which will encourage artists, those which will develop appreciation and enjoyment of the arts by citizens and those which will affect localities. How one does all this should be a matter of interpretation.

The NEA chose around 1970 to celebrate the congressional impulse rather than to argue with it. The statement of Nancy Hanks before the authorizing committee in 1973 set the tone for all the future meetings between Congress and this division of the Executive branch. It stated that great and direct benefits

could be expected from NEA funding—that citizens would be measurably improved morally. It stated that enormous numbers of peoples and associations benefitted from, participated in agency programs. And NEA, behind the scenes, acted to garner as many congressional or local statements as possible about the direct utility of the arts for citizenship.
acted to garner as many congressional or local statements as possible about the direct utility of the arts for citizenship.

By adopting Congress' own argument, NEA found itself in a predicament. On the one hand, it argued for professionalism, for the support of good arts institutions, and for the eventual equivalent of State Opera in several of the arts. On the other hand, it wanted to appease Congress, and to distribute funds evenly to mass audiences. There was really only one way to solve the impasse, which was to practice the strategy which has since 1970 been a constant in NEA discourse: to hold out the hope that some day appropriations would be half a billion dollars each year. This might have allowed all contradictions to be resolved: not only would all applications be eligible for award; money would be available for the ministerial projects and subsidies.

When that sum was awarded the agency would have escaped the bind of identifying but not pursuing the public interest. And it certainly might have worked, if the money came forth. But if the half-billion remains mythological, then the NEA is stuck with a budget about one-third that amount, and a strategy which for that figure is unworkable.

We go back to that office of the General Counsel and what it might have done. It might, as in the case of NEH, reserved more of the budget for professional purposes. It might have drawn up a list of priorities and put money aside for them. Above all, it might have made clear that, while social benefits did ensue from the support of art, they were not as important as the support of art. And that *constituent* and *public interests* ought to be distinguished.

The *public* interest in the arts if often opposed by *constituent* interest—which speak in the name of the public. In such cases the public interest will rarely prevail: no one, after all, knows who the public is or where it may be reached, while we all know that constituent representatives are highly visible. But perhaps the main point should be this: it is customary to identify the constituency with the public, to accept the former's representative quality. Yet the constituency and the public are two very different groups.

Broadly speaking, the effectiveness of any agency is to be judged by its freedom of action. A quantifiable sense of its effectiveness can be discerned in annual budgets. Where there are line-items, that is, instructions by Congress to reward those who do not have to apply for funds, there are corresponding subtractions of initiative. For example, NEA must give one-fifth of its annual budget to State Arts Councils, and about one-twentieth to the American Film Institute. It is possible that such funds will be well used, but reviews of their expenditure indicate the opposite. If effectiveness is a criterion, then it must be recognized that the agency does not have control over one-quarter of its budget. Like entitlements in larger agencies, line-items prevent making decisions. They indicate the last step in a familiar process: one which begins with identifying the public interest, which proceeds to serve that interest through some finite organization and which culminates in a relationship with constituencies expecting annual support. One expects then to find some confusion about the meaning of "public interest"; and one is not surprised to find a good deal of it about "art" itself.

CHAPTER XIII

What the Humanities Do

In this concluding chapter I would like to take up some of those things which cause the same kind of misinterpretation of the humanities that obtains in the arts. I am going to organize what I have to say around a specific report on the humanities. And my own ideas about what the humanities are and what they should do will be both explicitly stated and, I am sure, implicitly understood.

In 1980 the Rockefeller Foundation sponsored a national report which was called *The Humanities in American Life*. The intention of this report was to affirm the importance of the humanities, and to call for support for them from private and public sources. The group producing this report was made up largely of educational administrators. From my point of view, its unique interest here is that the report describes itself as the successor to that of the 1964 Commission on the Humanities. I began this book by describing that 1964 report and it will, I think, be useful to end by noting certain changes and comparisons.

As we recall, in 1964, it was possible unselfconsciously to believe that the disciplines of the humanities were professional. They were studied by experts and taught to students. If they had social benefits that lay in the improvement of intelligence, not in the solution of national problems directly. The study of literature or of language, it had been acknowledged from Cardinal Newman on, did not make men better or more reasonable; it only made them more able. So that, like education itself, the study of humanities was a kind of intermediate accomplishment, giving us only the hope of moral advancement through rational training.

My own business in managing NEH was, I thought, to keep the humanities professional while making their benefits available to the public. Scholars could do the scripts for something like the *Adams Family Chronicle* and the public could enjoy good television. Art experts could arrange for the organization and interpretation of an exhibition on French Impressionism, and the public could enjoy museums even more unreservedly. What I should not do, I thought, was to redefine the humanities as in themselves sources of direct public benefit, or give to constituencies or pressure groups funds in the name of the humanities. That would have been to follow the example of the Arts Endowment, which is much less concerned with the creation of actual works of art then with the satisfaction of those who become its beneficiaries.

But there does seem to be some large-scale redefinition at work, at least if the 1980 report is taken into consideration. Large sentiments are being expressed and large promises are made—and they resemble the discourse which a political agency reserves for its constituency. In the report, the humanities take upon themselves those benefits which have been least thoughtfully ascribed to the arts. In the report, as in the congressional hearings of 1973 which I have described, the study of the humanities, like that of the arts, makes us better, more moral, less susceptible to war or poverty, even nicer people.

Let us examine some ideas directly. We are told at the beginning that the humanities

> . . . tell us about ourselves, stretch our imagination, and enrich our experience. They increase our distinctively human potential.
>
> The humanities presume particular methods of expression and inquiry—language, dialogue, reflection, imagination, and metaphor. In the humanities the aims of these activities of mind are not geometric proof and quantitative measure, but rather insight, perspective, critical understanding, discrimination and creativity. These aims are not unique to the humanities, but are found in other fields, in images from the arts, and in new forms of expression created by film, television, and computers.

The aim of the report is evidently inclusiveness, which it may have accomplished at the cost of accuracy. Whatever "human potential" may be, its increase is not the end of education. I am going to have to guess that some moral end is implied by that phrase, even some kind of hope which is religious or political. Possibly, the inspiration for the use of that phrase comes from the literature of self-help. At any event, nowhere among these aims is the production of intelligence stated.

There are two other things that I think are remarkable in this passage. The first has to do with that glowing, positive, and meaningless phrase about books which "enrich our experience." The notion is that books are literally reflective; telling us not about *themselves* but of *ourselves*. Their end is to please, fulfill or "enrich" the customer. That is to say that books have few ideas—and that they do not themselves have a quarrel with life. I think it plain that the function of some books—those by Swift, Kafka and Hemingway—is to wound. They deride our "human potential." Second, it is of enormous interest to see that the humanities share their ends with film, television and computers. Possibly the thought is expressed because film, television and computers are popular, while humanities are not: perhaps the idea is that popularity can be influenced or translated by the power of suggestion. But of course these things are not the same as modes of humanistic study or of humanistic expression. They are good, they are useful, but they are different. They may in fact be new forms of expression, but they depend on ideas to express. The ballooning of definition, the urge to include everything so that the offensive process of discriminating against some things need not be undertaken, seem plainly conscious.

Let us look at another passage, this one concerned more with pieties than with unmade distinctions:

> The essence of the humanities is a spirit or an attitude toward humanity . . . They base their education on sus-

> taining principles of personal enrichment and civic responsibility. . . . They can approach questions of value, no matter how complex, with intelligence and goodwill.

I believe that what the passage praises is law, not the humanities. And I think it might be said that the "essence" of the humanities is not charity: *it is style*. Humanistic discourse is rarely disinterested. It is a matter of intellectual adversary proceedings. It is Johnsonian, conducted by wit and prejudice well expressed. It is, in short, *argument*. It is often biased. If the humanities are to be defined as books or ideas which "enrich" or make their audience responsible, then they have no place for the great minds of unreason. But surely Auden has said it best: poetry makes nothing happen. It does not allow us to approach questions of value without passionate and wrongheaded intensity. It certainly does not promote goodwill. On the contrary, cultivated intelligence is accustomed to masking its resentment. And, surely few have in fact ever approached a moral issue with "goodwill." We reserve for moral issues the normal combination of prejudice and righteousness. That is why we have courts as well as libraries.

If the report is to make us more moral, it seems also bent on making us more scientific. Part of the argument of the report is that the humanities are like the arts; and another part suggests that they are really like technology:

> We all need to understand the characteristics of scientific research. We must all learn something about the use of media and of new technologies for storing, transmitting, and expanding knowledge. Without this sort of literacy, our society as a whole will be less able to apply science and technology to humanistic needs, less able to measure the human effects of scientific achievement, less able to judge the information we produce and receive. Our schools and colleges have no higher duty than to sharpen these critical senses, which are inseparable from the humanities.

This passage ends a long section of recommendations that the humanities attach themselves to the physical sciences. It seems to be motivated by the desire to shelter under the rock of success. While some good can be done by exploring ethics, values and methods of scientific inquiry there is no reason to assume that the humanities are born to comment on the sciences. And many readers may object to the idea that education in the humanities has "no higher duty" than to develop the ability to evaluate media or science. It is much to be feared that this time around the commission included no philosophers, for from the time of Plato on contemplation as well as action has been part of the examined life. Possibly the highest duty is self-knowledge.

Because I was one of the founders of the movement to support the study of biomedical ethics and other social issues of scientific development I think that I can recognize certain hankerings in this report. The Humanities Endowment, the National Science Foundation, and other institutions cooperated in the study of the effects of scientific discovery. It was important to do so: to establish at least some expectations about the changes that technology would make in our lives. But the business of the humanities is not to become an appendage of the sciences. The humanities have their own agenda.

The humanities cannot, I almost regret to say, make us better citizens. It is the great misconception of our time that doing things that are good for us, we become good. Possibly the heart of the report is revealed when it discusses the results of education in the liberal arts:

> Our schools must prepare young people for competent and informed participation in community life and for the greatest possible degree of fulfillment in private life. These are not possible without the humanities. . . . One learns to value cultural tradition and change, active citizenship and private contemplation. . . . Administrators and humanists must assert that essential goals of education depend on the humanities—the development of

> citizens who can make informed and critical judgments, and the enrichment of individual life.

First, some notes on language: there are no more humanists. The last one, possibly, was Samuel Johnson, who united dogmatic and orthodox Christian ethics to the study of texts. And, a mind like Johnson's would have recoiled from words like "fulfillment" and, yet once more, "enrichment." The passage represents another retreat from intelligence. It asserts that the end of humanistic education is not only the pursuit but the actual capture of happiness. But, as Ronald Gottesman has put the matter, "The study of medicine does not ensure good health. . . . The study of psychiatry does not ensure freedom from neurosis. . . . Reading, even mastering, great religious, literary, or philosophic texts is not a guarantor of morally superior behavior." Or, as William F. Buckley, Jr. has put the matter, he would rather be governed by the first four hundred names in the Boston directory than by the faculty of Harvard.

If the preceding passage validates the humanities by their connection to what we *really* respect—that is, the sciences—then this passage connects them to what we *really* love, ourselves. It suggests that human society is the measure of all things. But surely the vision of human society expressed is that of a bee-hive: industrious, disciplined, full of right-thinking. It is quite possible that the end of education is the capacity to enjoy the printed page. And was it not Shakespeare who said that the profit of learning language might be the ability to curse?

Finally, a pair of passages which indicate that possibly more than the desire to make the support of humanities attractive to donors public and private is at work. One of the great and inherent problems of democracy is that all things become valued by utilitarianism. So that the report can say, with confidence, that,

> The humanities bring to life the ideal of cultural pluralism. . . . They leaven the stable values of citizenship. . . . Many young people today lack confidence in the future,

> their precocious cynicism reflecting our failure to solve persistent social problems and our growing awareness of limited material resources. In times of economic uncertainty, young people are often urged to prepare for earning a livelihood and discouraged from studying the humanities. We can ill afford to starve the spirit that moves each younger generation to search for humane solutions to perennial human problems.

I don't think that the humanities have much to do with cultural pluralism. They originated in the defense of Renaissance Christian society. Most humanists were doctrinaire and either inflicted or suffered imprisonment and death for their ideas, from Servetus to John Bunyan. The report finds it as difficult to grapple with the Renaissance idea of the humanities as the Arts Endowment finds it difficult to grapple with the Renaissance idea of patronage. The former idea seems to be that everything matters equally while the latter seems to mean that art patronage is designed to benefit the widest and least critical public constituency. Renaissance patronage of art, so often invoked in the halls of Congress by the NEA, was a matter of aristocratic taste. And humanism was a movement tightly associated with the church, and promoted by scholars who were ministers of state. It was a highly aggressive intellectual movement, one which assumed that Christian social values were the end of the good life. Most humanists were about as tolerant of "cultural pluralism" as John Milton who thought the idea complete nonsense.

"Cultural pluralism" is invoked here, however, because America has now been broken down into conflicting political constituencies, each of which is convinced that its ideas must either dominate or share public power. The virtue evidently lies in asserting that the values of minorities racial or sexual, or of any competing groups or associations, need not fear evaluation.

By now one sees that the humanities have become interpreted in as instrumental a way as the arts. They help us to understand science. They help us understand politics. They make us better. And they relieve the cynicism of the young. But there are holes in this argument big enough to drive the proverbial Mack truck through. For example, if human problems are in fact perennial, how can we be responsible for forestalling them? The "persistent" problem may simply be a historical fact. And there is little that either art or humanities can do for those who "lack confidence." In fact, we may enter where angels fear to tread, imposing half-baked ideas derived from self-help and self-fulfillment manuals, taking over the work of religion, secularizing every evil by assuming that it is a "problem."

Finally, another adjuration as problems are secularized and culture is sacralized:

> Each major branch of the humanities helps educate men and women for citizenship. History provides clues for understanding the present. Literature broadens personal moral vision through exploring character, circumstance, and choice. Philosophy supplies rules of analysis and criteria for belief.

Speaking of literature and moral choice, let us not forget The Man Who Liked Dickens. The idea of a more orderly life through literature—a life of "choice," "rules" and "belief"—goes back a long way, possibly to the indoctrination practiced by Thomas Arnold at Rugby which produced a thousand Christian gentlemen and a generation of anti-semites. Possibly the humanities are to be valued because they question social ideas, not because they exemplify them.

We have been reminded by Lionel Trilling in *Beyond Culture* that modernism is a subversive enterprise. Its authors—Lawrence and Yeats and Joyce—are hostile to social earnestness. I suppose we ought to remember that there are really two examples of the kinds of relationships possible between the writer and the state: one is Petrarch, crowned with laurel; but the other is Socrates, indicted for insufficient piety. I don't think that the argument will do: literature is eventually self-justifying. As for educating men and women for citizenship, we have followed that pattern rather precisely for two generations now. It seems, at least in the secondary schools, not to have worked. In fact, the values of citizenship seem often to have been opposed to those of intelligence.

I hope then, to end not cynically but realistically; to have indicated that there are many pitfalls in thinking about the right relationship of ideas to the state, and of cultural benefits to the public. Politics is always eager to have the services of culture. But culture, in the service of politics, is no longer itself.

INDEX